Raising the Dead

Raising the Dead

A Doctor Encounters the Miraculous

CHAUNCEY W.
CRANDALL IV, MD

NEW YORK   BOSTON   NASHVILLE

Copyright © 2010 by Chauncey W. Crandall IV, MD

The author is represented by Yates & Yates, Attorneys & Literary Agents.

FaithWords
Hachette Book Group
237 Park Avenue
New York, NY 10017

Visit our website at www.faithwords.com

Printed in the United States of America

First Edition: September 2010
10 9 8 7 6 5 4 3 2 1

FaithWords is a division of Hachette Book Group, Inc.
The FaithWords name and logo are trademarks of Hachette Book Group, Inc.

Library of Congress Cataloging-in-Publication Data

Crandall, Chauncey W.
   Raising the dead : a doctor encounters the miraculous / Chauncey W. Crandall,
IV.—1st ed.
     p. cm.
   ISBN 978-0-446-55720-7
   1. Crandall, Chauncey W.   2. Cardiologists—United States—Biography.
3. Christian physicians—United States—Biography.   4. Miracles.   5. Spiritual
healing.   I. Title.
   RC666.72.C73A3 2010
   616.1'20092—dc22
   [B]   2009035045

*To my wife, Deborah, my sons Christian and Chad,
and for "my Indians," the patients the Lord has entrusted to my care.
All to the glory of God.*

Contents

Beginning in the Middle:
An Introduction

This is the story of a doctor, a skeptical scientist by nature, who came to believe in supernatural healing. It's the story of how a Yale-trained physician and cardiologist learned about God's heart—the way its beating gives life and sustains us even in the worst of times. It's my story.

It's a lot more than my story, too, because the miracles that have taken place before my eyes and underneath my hands are evidence not only of God's healing power but of God's intention, through Jesus Christ, to save and eventually heal everyone. God is at work restoring all things. It's an ultimate promise. Even death cannot defeat God's power, as I've seen through watching more than one person be raised from the dead: tremendous miracles that are signs of every believer's resurrection to eternal life—the ultimate miracle.

Every story has a beginning, middle, and end, but not necessarily in that order, as the saying goes. Many stories begin in the middle of things as this one does. It begins with a man being raised from the dead, a miracle in which I played a significant part. This astounding event was used by God to open up many new avenues of service and ministry, and in ways I could never have anticipated it brought my own story to prominence. It's often what people know about me.

My role in the miracle cannot be understood, though, apart from how I learned to join God in His healing work—and in the real, spiritual battle of this life—through seeking healing for my son when he became desperately ill with leukemia. That's why the quest for my son's healing follows right on the heels of the account of this widely known miracle, as an explanation of how I was prepared to see people raised from the dead.

The hard, even crucifying, lessons that I learned through my son's illness taught me to recognize evil when I saw it and join Christ in His fight against it. I was a believer long before my son became ill, but I didn't really see life for the spiritual battle it is or know how to fight the battle. Through my son's illness I learned how "to put on the whole armor of God"—how to use the spiritual exercises and disciplines that God gives us.

Once I found myself on the front lines, I learned to fight as hard and fast as I possibly could. I sought every gift God could give me. I went from being a run-of-the-mill believer to being a radicalized Christian. This did not make me a humorless fanatic. It actually gave me joy and delight in doing God's work.

Once I committed myself to remaining at Christ's side despite the most devastating loss any parent can know, God began using me to assure people of His salvation through a double-healing ministry: I began offering my patients and those I met through speaking engagements the best of Christ and the best of medicine.

Some Christian readers may already be tempted to pigeonhole this story as "charismatic" or "Pentecostal." Non-Christian readers may wonder whether I really have the credentials I claim. I invite the skeptics to look up my medical board certifications.

I would ask evangelical and other Christians to consider whether the whole church should not be considered "charismatic," in the sense of being sustained through God's "gifts," His "charisma." The whole church must also be "pentecostal," born at Pentecost through the power of the Holy Spirit. I cannot deny that I have been influenced by these particular strains of Christianity—nor would I want to. And every strain of Christianity has its own particular vocabulary, some of which you will encounter here, although I've tried to keep the "church talk" to a minimum. But I think that any believer or even non-Christian who gives my story half a chance will find a meaning that is faithful to Jesus's teaching and His work—to His good news. Few "Pentecostal" books take sufficient account of the Cross, for example. My story would be meaningless without it.

Let what I've experienced—my eyewitness testimony—speak for itself. Please suspend judgment until you've heard the whole story. It's not something I could have possibly made up.

Raising the Dead

*Why should any of you consider it incredible that
God raises the dead?*
—Acts 26:8

CHAPTER I

"Shock Him One More Time"—Raising the Dead

On October 20, 2006, a heavyset fifty-three-year-old man with red hair walked through the entrance of the emergency room at the Palm Beach Gardens Hospital and approached the admissions desk. Earlier that morning, suffering from an upset stomach and sweat-inducing anxiety, he had called a fellow mechanic to tell him he'd be late to work and headed for the ER. On the way he began experiencing chest pain and shortness of breath. A big, powerful guy, he had a hawkish look, his eyes keen and watchful. But as he told the nurse his name, Jeff Markin, and described his symptoms, he looked as if he were about to become the prey of a descending terror: his eyes bulged and he began breathing more quickly through a half-opened mouth.

He fumbled out his wallet to retrieve his insurance ID card, then collapsed in a heap, his head smacking the linoleum floor. The female security guard rushed over and cradled him, praying for his life, while the nurse at the reception desk summoned emergency personnel, who came running.

I was in another part of the hospital, the operating room wing, where I had what we call a "runway" of patients prepped for angioplasties, stent insertions, heart catheterizations, intra-aortic balloon pumps, and pacemakers. Each patient had a family waiting to know the outcome and their loved one's prognosis. So when I heard over the hospital intercom "Code blue," which indicated a cardiopulmonary emergency, and my name being called—"Dr. Chauncey Crandall...Dr. Chauncey Crandall...Please report immediately"—I was not eager to head for the ER. As the senior cardiologist on duty, my job is to ensure that the emergency room physician and his team have done everything possible on the patient's behalf and make a final assessment of the case. When I was younger, I used to run to such emergencies, but now, in middle age and with more trust in my colleagues, I walk. To tell the truth, I was hoping the case would be resolved by the time I arrived, even if that meant the worst.

When I arrived, the emergency room where the code team was treating Jeff looked like a war zone. The physician on duty had pulled in all available personnel. The patient's blood work for the standard Toponin I test had been run to the lab, although there was little doubt from the electrocardiogram results that he had suffered an acute myocardial infarction—a massive heart attack. Nurses ran two IV lines, administering standard drugs—ASA (aspirin), heparin, a beta-blocker, and thrombolytics to dissolve clots. Jeff was bagged to get some oxygen into his lungs, but when that didn't work he was quickly intubated and hooked up to a ventilator, and a nasogastric tube was inserted to clear his stomach of air and secretions. The ER physician ordered atropine and epinephrine injected to aid the beating of the patient's heart. In Jeff's case, ventricular fibrillation—the irregular beating of his heart at hyperspeed—was quickly followed by cardiac arrest; he flatlined.

The ECG electrodes on the patient's upper torso were cleared so that he could be shocked with the defibrillator—the paddles everyone's seen on television. "Clear!" *Wham!* The shock was so intense it caused Jeff's body to jump above the stretcher. By the time I arrived, the team had shocked the patient six times, and I watched them administer the seventh. The doctors and nurses had already been working on the patient for nearly forty minutes. I noticed that his head, especially his lips, and his fingers and toes were cyanotic—black with death from lack of oxygen. When cyanosis appears, there's little hope. His arms lolled at either side of the examination table; his pupils were dilated and fixed; he had been down for too long. The ER physician asked me for my assessment, looking for confirmation of what everyone in that room already knew.

Once I arrived on the scene, I had begun to root for the patient and the heroic fight the ER team was waging for his life. But the appropriate conclusion was unavoidable: it was time to call the Code on the patient, declaring the time of his death, according to advanced cardiac life support (ACLS) protocol. Jeff Markin was officially declared dead at 8:05 a.m.

Once the Code was ended, the doctors and nurses in the room left quickly. No one likes to hang around death—the sight and smell are repulsive. I still had to write up my final assessment, which I did on a small table at one side of the room. Only one nurse remained, who was in charge of preparing the body for his family to see and processing by the morgue. She removed the tubes from his throat and the IVs from his arms, then began sponging off the yellow stains of antiseptic and traces of blood.

With my report complete, I headed toward the door and back to my runway of patients. Before I crossed its threshold, however, I sensed God was telling me to turn around and pray for that man. This seemed foolish—an idle thought caused by the stress of the situation or even mischievous influence. But then my sense of God telling me this occurred a second time and more forcefully. But what would I pray? And to what purpose? I did not know this man, and, frankly, I felt embarrassed by the impulse to pray for him. But I knew that when I had ignored such impulses in the past I never felt at peace afterward.

I stood beside the body, and although the words I said came through me, I had no sense of devising them. It was more as if I were God's intercom, relaying a "divine code." "Father God," I said, under my breath, "I cry out for this man's soul. If he does not know You as his Lord and Savior, raise him from the dead now, in Jesus' name."

The nurse gave me a look that said, *You are weird!*

Then something happened that *was* truly weird. Of its own accord my right arm shot up as if to catch a gift from above, in a gesture of prayer and praise. I didn't feel much of anything, and yet I knew that God had entered the scene in a surprising way.

At that moment, the ER doctor walked back into the room, and I pointed to the patient and said, "Shock this man one more time."

"Dr. Crandall," he said in disbelief, "I can't shock the patient one more time. I've shocked him again and again. He's dead."

"Please, for me," I said, "shock him one more time."

He looked at me, puzzled, as if he might need to call in a psychiatrist. But, thinking it best to humor me first, he did as I asked. *Boom!*

Blip...blip...blip. The remaining ECG leads registered a

heartbeat. *A perfect heartbeat!* About seventy-five of them a minute, in a perfectly normal rhythm. In my more than twenty years as a cardiologist, I have never seen a heartbeat restored so completely and suddenly—a heart that restarts usually beats irregularly if not erratically before it settles into a normal rhythm.

I looked at Jeff Markin. His abdomen started to tremble and move and then his chest started to rise and fall. He was breathing on his own! Then his black, cyanotic fingers twitched. Next his toes. In almost no time he was mumbling.

The nurse screamed—a long, piercing wail right out of the movies. "Doctor," she asked, "what have you done? What are we supposed to do?" She was not only terrified but angry, her face red and blotchy. This was not a miracle to her, as I found out later, but more like the creation of Frankenstein. She couldn't be expected to handle a situation like this. *What was she to do?*

"Let's get him into ICU," I said. "Immediately. *Now!*"

CHAPTER 2

The Unspoken Question

While suffering from cardiogenic shock, Jeff fully stabilized in the ICU, and I was able to entrust his care to another physician over the weekend. When I looked in on him on Monday, Jeff was sitting up in his bed *talking*. He might have been mistaken for another person, except that his fingers and toes were still cyanotic, bruised by death.

That morning the nurse who was cleaning Jeff up when he came back to life came running up to me to explain why she had been not only terrified but angry. "I was so mad at you, Dr. Crandall. I thought he'd be brain-dead, but now look at him!" She went on to express her complete amazement at his recovery. Eventually, she stopped talking and stared at me, her eyes searching mine. I could see that she wanted to ask me a question that she could not voice. All I could say was, "We have a great God, don't we?"

The nurse's unstated question, I would guess, is the one many of my colleagues harbor. How does a doctor, a cardiologist—a man of science—come to believe in praying for healing, to the point of asking God to raise a man from the dead? That I now complement the best of traditional medicine with praying for my patients is a scandal.

Why I Began Running After God

I was a Christian, but a conventional one who kept his faith and his profession mostly separate, until June 2000. Late one night as my wife, Deborah, and I were about to go to bed, I received a phone call from the hospital's testing lab. "Dr. Crandall," the lab technician said, "we have an alert value that we need to let you know about. The patient's white [blood cell] count is very high."

"How high?"

"Over eighty thousand."

Anything over ten thousand is abnormal. *That guy's dead,* I thought. He had leukemia. "Well, who is the patient?"

"Dr. Crandall," the technician said, "it's your son Chad."

The shock made my whole body go limp. My face probably went ashen, as Deborah gave me a look that asked, *What's going on?*

"Are you sure? You have the right patient?"

"Yes, Dr. Crandall, we've checked it many times. I'm so sorry."

Our boys, eleven-year-old fraternal twins, Chad and Christian, were our lives. Chad was a flaxen-haired sprite, with blue eyes and freckles. Christian was dark-haired, olive-skinned. Both were avid tennis players and competed in area tournaments. They were complementary in almost every way. While Christian was the natural leader, Chad was the shy charmer, the one everyone wanted to be around once they came to know him. *How could Chad be dying?* At that moment, he and his brother were sleeping in their room.

Chad had been hydrating more than usual, consuming a ton of cranberry juice. But *dying?* I was so shaken I couldn't collect my thoughts. I couldn't even exactly recall why Deborah had taken him in for blood work.

When I hung up, Deborah asked, "What's wrong?"

"There's a problem with a patient and I have to go" was all I said. I didn't want to tell her about Chad's condition until I knew more, although what I expected to learn at that time of night I couldn't say. I simply went into action.

I walked out and got in my car and started hyperventilating. "What's going on, Lord?" I prayed. "Why Chad?" For the next half hour or so I called every hematologist I knew, the blood doctors who could give me a better assessment of what the test results indicated. The only one I was able to contact was the one nearest at hand, my neighbor down the street, Dr. Robert Jacobson. I asked if I could come by.

By this time it was well after eleven, and Dr. Jacobson greeted me in his pajamas. "Robert, they say Chad has leukemia. You have to help me, because I just can't make sense of this, I can't think." The fear was so strong my vision tunneled and I couldn't hold on to a thought, as one chaotic idea followed another.

Robert kindly called the hospital lab and spoke with the technician. My friend confirmed the news, but he couldn't tell me much more. He helped set up an appointment the next day with the hospital's head pediatrician, Dr. MacArthur. "Like everyone else," Robert said, counseling me, "you are going to have to take this one step at a time."

About midnight I arrived back home, where Deborah met me at the door. "I've never seen you like this. Is it something with the practice? Did somebody make a mistake?"

"Deborah, they say Chad has leukemia."

She put her hand to her mouth, stifling screams, and went straight out to the backyard. There was a full moon that night, a soft breeze, and she stayed out there for hours. She prayed over and over again: "Lord, this can't be true. This can't be true!"

I watched her from a distance, not knowing how to comfort her or whether she wanted me to right then. I'm not sure either of us actually went to sleep that night.

When the boys came down for breakfast the next morning, I saw what I had avoided seeing for the last couple of months. Chad was thin, pale. His brother was a good two inches taller, something I had chalked up to uneven growth spurts. But then I remembered sitting on the couch by Chad and noticing that he had lost muscle tone in his arms, something that didn't make any sense for an eleven-year-old tennis fanatic. I had guessed he must be overdoing it—the weight loss the result of the Florida June heat. But now I saw how everything added up, including his outsized thirst, and I finally realized that he was as seriously ill as the test indicated. My fear turned to anguish.

Deborah and I explained to the boys that we needed to go see the doctor that morning. Deborah took Chad aside and explained in slightly more detail, trying not to frighten him.

Following his examination of Chad, all four of us went into Dr. MacArthur's private office for the consultation. He did not mince words. Chad had leukemia. The exact type had yet to be determined. They would have to do a much more extensive blood workup. Chad would probably need a bone marrow transplant.

9

Until then, he would be put on chemotherapy—a drug then known as hydroxyurea (now called hydroxycarbamide)—to get his blood counts under control. If his counts went any higher, Chad would have to be put in the hospital.

The diagnosis shocked both our sons. Another boy in the area had died of leukemia, and our sons knew more than most children their age how deadly the disease could be. Chad reacted by tuning out, but Christian convulsed with dry heaves, and we were all soon in the bathroom trying to calm him.

When we returned to the house that night, I looked over at the piano and saw a Bible on the music stand above the keyboard. I held it in the air and prayed, *"Lord, if You are real, You have to heal my son."*

This prayer was more of a turning point than I could have known. As a doctor I knew that we were not looking at a good outcome. I could only rely on my Christian faith, one unprepared to meet such a challenge. Until my son became ill, I was content to know that I was going to heaven, and for the rest I depended on my own ability to meet any challenge, as well as the common sense that my family instilled. "I will find a way" was my motto. For the first time in my life I was up against an enemy that was completely beyond my control.

The only thing we had experienced in our marriage that was like this experience in any way was ten years earlier when Deborah and I tried to have children to no avail. We took the boys' finally coming into our lives as a miracle—there's a story there, too. We held them as tightly as we could and were no doubt overprotective.

But now *leukemia* shattered any thought of going on as before. Deborah's faith was deeper than mine; she had helped bring me to

Christianity, in fact. Over the years she had encountered the reality of healing prayer on a couple of occasions, as well as other evidences of God's continuing presence in the world. I didn't know much, but I knew enough to follow those bread crumbs of faith to their source. I knew enough to ask God that my son be healed. And so began a new way of life.

Skirmishes as the Battle Begins

During the next weeks I cut my work schedule down radically in order to become an expert in the treatment of leukemia and what the Bible says about healing. Looking back, I wish I'd had Christian friends who could have interceded with me for my son's healing; Christian friends who really believed, as I do now, that we fight not only against "flesh and blood," or natural causes, as the apostle Paul wrote, but against "principalities, against powers, against the rulers of the darkness of this world," meaning the forces of evil (Eph. 6:12 KJV). I'm convinced that cancer is not only a disease but a purposeful evil. But at that point I did not even know how to interpret the Bible properly.

I began by reading through the New Testament and underlining every passage that had to do with healing. Then I did computer searches throughout the Bible, cross-referencing passages to see when and how and for what purpose God chose to bring healing through prayer. I also began to read books like T. L. Osborn's *Healing the Sick*, Reinhard Bonnke's *Mighty Manifestations*, and Charles and Frances Hunter's *How to Heal the Sick*.

At the same time I called old colleagues at Yale and Duke and other places around the country to find out where the best pediatric

11

cancer centers were and the latest developments in the field. Subsequent tests on Chad, a bone marrow aspirate and a bone marrow biopsy, along with the FISH lab test, revealed that he had a form of leukemia known as chronic myelogenous leukemia (CML). CML is comparatively rare in children.

Looking back, what I should've done was find the best doctor, entrust Chad to his care, and then spend time in the Word and seek God. But I wanted to do everything I could, which to my mind meant serving as lead doctor in the case, particularly when it came to shielding the family from the bad news about CML and its likely progress.

My attempts to protect the family would later cause strife, as I unwittingly became the face of the disease—the one who was always disappointing their hopes. At the time, "I will find a way" took over wherever it could.

Chad's counts did go up, unhappily, and we had to put him in the hospital so that his chemotherapy regimen could be strengthened. Our friends who attended a nearby church came by and suggested that we bring him to the Wednesday evening service for prayer. I doubted his doctors would release him, but Deborah insisted: "You tell the doctor we are taking our son to the service." She had the greater wisdom, and in this and many instances to follow she rightly pointed out when it was time for us to take charge of Chad's care.

The doctor resisted, as I knew he would, since Chad had an IV. I had to tell him, "Listen, I'm taking my son to church tonight. We're seeking God."

Then I had to persuade Chad that he needn't be embarrassed about going to church with an IV hookup, which we covered to minimize his uneasiness.

In the middle of the Wednesday night service, the pastor called all the elders to gather around Chad, lay hands on him, and pray for him, as the pastor anointed him with oil. It was a straightforward evangelical church, and this ministration of healing prayer, although it's thoroughly biblical (James 5:14), was an unusual event in the church's practice. Deb and I were grateful. I wept as the pastor and the elders prayed. I just needed some reassurance from the Lord that He was there, helping us.

Afterward, Chad looked better, and sure enough when the hospital checked his counts the next morning, they were down enough for him to come home.

My study of the Scriptures began convincing me that my son could be healed through prayer. One key seemed to be a community of believers uniting their prayers toward this end. This was certainly the case at the Wednesday night service at the church.

I didn't feel, though, that many of the Christians within our circle actually believed in the power of prayer to heal. Everyone readily volunteered to pray for Chad, that's true, but when I asked whether spiritual gifts like healing were as active today as in the time of the New Testament, I ran into demurrals. Many thought the miraculous times of the Scriptures had passed. The miracles had been necessary as a witness before the New Testament came into existence. In our time, the Word of God sufficed for belief, and therefore miraculous healing was rare, if it existed at all.

But I didn't see in the Bible where a time limit was placed on the power of healing prayer. Maybe I didn't want to see this because my son was sick, but why would Christ suspend His promise to His followers that they would do "greater" miracles than His own (John 14:12)?

Deborah and I were coming to believe more and more in the

13

reality of the supernatural in our own time, and we became willing to take measures that I'm sure in many of our fellow Christians' eyes looked suspicious. Simultaneously, we reached out to the best doctors in the world and took unusual paths in our family's quest for healing through Christ.

CHAPTER 3

Seeing Life, Seeing Death

A short time later Chad was scheduled for an appointment at the Dana-Farber Cancer Institute in Boston—part of the Harvard medical complex—when a friend called to say that Sister Briege McKenna, a nun with an international Christian ministry, was staying on Palm Beach island. She was willing to pray for Chad, but she could see him only on the day we were flying out.

Once crippled with rheumatoid arthritis, Sister Briege was healed at the age of twenty-four while praying during worship. A short time later she was given the gift of healing through prayer, and she has been involved in this ministry for thirty years. After reading her book, *Miracles Do Happen*, people come from all over the world to her retreat center in Tampa, Florida, to pray with her for healing. Deborah saw the opportunity for Sister Briege to pray with Chad as a gift we could not afford to pass up.

I was more intent on getting Chad to Dana-Farber on time. I

knew how fast his leukemia was progressing and understood too well the insidious nature of the disease.

CML is like a "mole" within an intelligence agency—it looks loyal while systematically working to undermine the body's defenses. With CML one bone marrow stem cell—just *one*—undergoes a chromosomal abnormality. Through other chromosomal activity a cancer gene forms and creates a protein that alters the white blood cells, red blood cells, and platelets that the stem cell manufactures. These cells are almost normal, but not quite—like the work of a traitorous agent. The affected white blood cells multiply at a much faster rate than normal and the red blood cells and platelets at a slower rate.

The affected red blood cells also don't do their job of carrying oxygen as effectively. The abnormal cells begin to crowd out the normal ones. The white blood cell count eventually rises so high that blood flow slows down like a freeway at rush hour and every system in the body is starved for oxygen. The patient becomes ever more anemic. That's why Chad's muscles and skin were wasting away, why he had trouble catching his breath, why he experienced night sweats, and why his spleen was swollen. That was why we had to get him to Dana-Farber *fast*!

"I Saw Jesus"

Deborah insisted we fit in the visit to Sister Briege. I saw how this would be possible only if I didn't go with them but remained at home to tie up the loose ends of our trip preparations on my own. I didn't like not going; I wanted to be there for Chad every step of the way.

Deborah took Chad to the residence of the Sugarcane family,

where Sister Briege was staying. Originally from Ireland, where she joined the Sisters of Saint Clare at fifteen, Sister Briege still reminds one of the Irish lass she once was, with thick, reddish-brown hair and the type of fair complexion that freckles in the sun. She has a broad, slightly gap-toothed smile and lines around her eyes that testify to her smile's frequent appearance. She wore a plain dress rather than a habit. As Deborah and Chad approached the house, she motioned and called out, "Come in, Chad, come in, Deborah, I want to pray for you."

She spoke briefly with Deborah and Chad about having a relationship with Christ, how the Lord can heal, and of the miracles she's seen. "When I pray for you, Chad," she said, "all I want for you to do is to think of Jesus." So she prayed for Chad to be healed, and when she finished, she said, "Whatever you do, just don't stop taking the medicine. That's what the Lord told me. Don't stop taking your medicine."

When Deborah and Chad came home, before we left for the airport, I had a private moment with Deborah in which I asked her how the visit with Sister Briege went. She gave me an answer I couldn't really believe. "When Sister Briege prayed for Chad," Deborah said, "I saw Christ."

"What?"

"I had my eyes closed, but as the sister was praying, I saw Christ walk into the room. He was dressed in a white gown. He was wearing a rope belt and sandals. I couldn't see His face. Just His hair and His body. But there was a peace and a presence about Him—I knew it was Jesus."

"But your eyes were closed."

"I don't care if my eyes were closed. I saw Jesus."

I didn't say anything, because how do you respond to that? I had my skeptical suspicions—the emotional circumstances, the power of autosuggestion.

After we arrived in Boston, driving to the hotel, I asked Chad about the visit with Sister Briege.

Deborah wanted to know, "Did you see anything?" They hadn't discussed Deborah's experience.

"Oh yeah, Mom," Chad said. "I saw Jesus."

"Okay," I said skeptically, "what did He look like? Give me details."

"I had my eyes closed, Dad, but I still saw Jesus. He had on a white gown and sandals, with a rope belt. I couldn't see His face, really."

The image they shared was a conventional one, I thought dismissively, and Sister Briege had asked them both to think of Jesus as she prayed. That they both noted Jesus wearing a rope belt gave me pause, though. That detail, while common enough, increased the likelihood of the vision's authenticity, as they both thought to mention it. Still, I wasn't about to get carried away.

"Something's Not Right"

The next morning, we kept our appointment at Dana-Farber Cancer Institute. A cancer center, even for a doctor, is a frightening place. It's hard to see people who have been reduced to skeletons walking around with IV poles. To glimpse others, particularly children, with their hair gone, limbs amputated, their heads sometimes grotesquely lopsided from craniectomies, is harrowing. The stench of death was rife in that place. And there was a darkened atmosphere at Dana-Farber that I still cannot account for—it could have been the shock of seeing so many people in the latter stages of their battle with cancer, of course, but I'm not sure it was only that.

We weren't in the building very long before Deborah wanted to leave. "We shouldn't stay here," she said. "I don't have a good feeling about this place."

"This is Harvard's cancer center," I said. "It's probably the best place in the world for the treatment of children. What are you talking about?"

"Something's not right," she said. She leaned over and whispered to me, "I feel like they are going to kill him."

"It's the cancer that's going to kill him if we don't get him treated!" I whispered right back. "This is our son. We have to do the best thing for him. I know it's hard."

Deborah stopped whispering. "I'm telling you, they will kill him. This place is evil. Let's leave now. I don't care about the appointment."

"Deborah, I'm a doctor. I have to meet with the doctors. I need to hear what they have to say. This is science, not voodoo."

She said, "I don't care what they say. I want to see what Jesus has to say about this."

"Deborah, please."

After we waited for more than an hour, we learned that we hadn't been properly scheduled. Somehow the person who set up the appointment hadn't communicated, and no one was prepared to take charge of Chad's case. The hospital staff knew it was in error and scrambled to make room for us. Still, we weren't going to be seeing the specialists I had found through my research, but their junior colleagues.

This first disappointment was the start of a long journey in which

I found out what it's really like to be on the receiving end of our medical system. I couldn't understand how they could be treating us this way. My son's life was on the line. I was a colleague—part of the medical brotherhood. I had spent a small fortune just flying the family to Boston. Chad needed the best of medical care—and our indifferent reception would only become more callous as the day unfolded.

A young woman finally met with us for a consultation. She was the type of specialist who seemed to believe that advanced training dispenses with a need for a bedside manner. Chad was right there by our sides as she launched into her evaluation, her tone so threatening she seemed to take the disease's side. "I'm sure you know CML is incurable. Very few make it, and that's even truer with children. You need to face the possibility that your son is going to die. That's the only way you'll be prepared for what he'll have to undergo in treatment."

Deborah started choking. She held out her hands for the doctor to stop. I tried to comfort her as best I could. I couldn't believe a physician would start off like this—not with the eleven-year-old patient in the room. Not in front of a patient of any age!

When Deborah recovered enough, she said, "You see! It's this place. It's *death*. Chad and I are going out into the hall. If you want to talk to this lady, you can."

Once Deborah and Chad had left, the young doctor continued in much the same way. She said that Chad needed a bone marrow transplant immediately. If we didn't set up the transplant, Chad was surely going to die. She couldn't promise the bone marrow transplant would be effective, but it would likely give us more time with him. We should use that time to get whatever affairs needed tending in order. I have never heard a physician speak so aggressively and ruthlessly, and she was talking about my son.

We Don't Want a Transplant

In fairness, part of this was motivated by Deborah's and my resistance to a bone marrow transplant. Most have heard of this as the magic cure, the silver bullet, for leukemia. As a doctor I was more aware than the average person of the risks. A bone marrow transplant is far from a slam dunk—a percentage of patients die from the procedure. Then there's graft-versus-host disease, which can cause numerous problems.

A bone marrow transplant involves wiping out the patient's immune system and the transfusion of bone marrow stem cells from someone who is a close match genetically. A perfect genetic match isn't wanted. The transplanted cells need to replace the patient's own cells, and a war ensues between the transplanted cells and those the body tries to regenerate. Even if the transplanted cells win out, this can come at a cost, described as graft-versus-host disease. The war between the cells can cause chronic skin disorders, liver failure, kidney failure—problems with just about every major system.

Children who receive bone marrow transplants become sterile and their growth is stunted. They can suffer gross disfigurement. I suppose it was a sign of our hopefulness that we still believed such a desperate remedy might be avoided. It was this hope that the young doctor was trying to check. I'm sure she thought Chad's parents, particularly his physician father, were foolishly resisting the one procedure that might save his life.

But I had brought Chad to Boston for remedies not available elsewhere. If we had wanted a bone marrow transplant, our facilities in Florida were perfectly suitable and far more convenient. The young doctor had nothing else to offer.

I walked out into the hall and said to Deborah, "You're right. Let's go home."

When we arrived back in Florida, I made a new agreement with my wife. "Deborah, I'm going to focus on the medical, and you focus on the spiritual. I'm having trouble doing both."

After that I stopped working almost entirely. All day, every day, I continued researching possible cures for CML, delving into cutting-edge studies, the latest drug trials, and calling every doctor and researcher on the forefront of the battle.

CHAPTER 4

A Miracle Drug or Miracles?

Before we moved to Palm Beach, I had been an assistant professor of medicine at the Medical College of Virginia (Richmond), where I had done consulting studies with Duke University Medicine. Duke's health-care complex includes an outstanding children's hospital as well as the university hospital. I thought Chad might receive better treatment there, and certainly a more thoughtful evaluation. Once again, the family flew with Chad to keep an appointment, this time in Durham, North Carolina.

I was thankful that we were received with more consideration, but there was still, I hate to admit, a Keystone Cops element. Our blood work was lost, and just as we were about to depart the whole family had to be retested. By this time we were giving more serious consideration to a bone marrow transplant, even though Chad's counts had been stabilized through chemotherapy and prayer. At Duke we discovered that Chad's brother, Christian, was an ideal candidate as a bone marrow donor, close enough as a fraternal twin but with sufficient genetic differences for his stem cells to replace Chad's in the graft-versus-host struggle. Still, when a transplant was recommended once more, we were hesitant.

Our indecision was partially a result of the fact that I was beginning to learn about the research of Dr. Brian Druker. He was on staff at both the Cancer Institute of Oregon Health & Science University and at the nearby Howard Hughes Medical Institute. He had previously been an instructor and researcher at Harvard, where he studied a family of signaling proteins that resulted in the abnormal formation of blood cells, especially the proliferation of white blood cells, as in Chad's CML. Dr. Druker discovered a way to detect the enzyme that led to this protein's creation. He also had good reason to believe that he had found a drug that turned off the enzyme. In the lab this drug was known as ST1571. Two years before, in 1998, Dr. Druker had conducted the first clinical trials on human beings with ST1571 and found that within six months every patient with CML, drawn from a pool of CML victims who had exhausted all other options, had gone into remission.[1] A 100 percent success rate is practically unknown in clinical trials—an amazing and incredibly promising result.

Dr. Druker proved to be as kind and caring as he was brilliant. During his time at Harvard, he had become restless spending all his time in the lab. He began devoting half of each day to treating patients at a community cancer clinic; that's how much he cared about people. He had moved to Oregon in 1993 to immerse himself in his patients' cases, even as his research continued. Within four or five weeks of Chad's diagnosis, we were off to Oregon to see him.

When we met with Dr. Druker, he said, "The recommendation is still the same—a bone marrow transplant. But the drug I've been working on, which is now called Gleevec, is undergoing trials at the FDA. I don't know how quickly it will be approved, or if it will be. I'm not promising anything. But it might be approved within the next year. Or we could try getting Chad entered in a future trial. Gleevec isn't a cure, but from the evidence to date, it might be what you are looking for. Most of the patients to whom it has been given have remained in remission. If we can get Chad on Gleevec, he won't need a bone marrow transplant and I believe he'll live." I could tell that Dr. Druker was now in the fight with us.

I don't know how high the plane was flying on the way home, but I was way above the clouds. I felt we had a possible solution in hand. I was still depending on Jesus, but I felt that this drug could be the means God would use to heal Chad or make CML a condition he could live with. Hadn't Sister Briege said, "Keep taking your medicine"? Perhaps this was the medicine she meant, because chemotherapy is not ordinarily described as "medicine," but Gleevec could be thought of that way—it came in pill form.

I immediately went on a quest to obtain Gleevec for Chad. I called everyone I knew who had anything to do with the world of cancer research and networked to see if I could get Chad into a trial. I made contacts in Europe where drugs are often available before they are approved in the United States. I asked the senior President Bush through political contacts to write a letter on behalf of Chad, which he was kind enough to do. I called the company developing the drug, Novartis, every week for additional updates: What's the FDA saying? When is it coming out? Are there any additional trials being run? How should Chad be prepared for possible inclusion? The Novartis people came to know me on a first-name basis. The quest for Gleevec continued through the fall of 2000 and the winter and spring of 2001.

Quest for Christ

As I mentioned, the first round of chemotherapy in Florida and our initial prayer sessions brought Chad's white blood cell count down. He started feeling better, gained back a few pounds, and had more energy. By September he was able to attend school and could even play tennis again, if on a reduced schedule.

As part of my effort to shield the family from dealing with doctors and callous medical personnel, I drew Chad's blood every week, ran it through the lab, and came home with the test results. This eventually made me, as I've mentioned, the face of the disease for the family, and I was more and more received—and avoided—like doom. But it was this or waiting for the phone to ring, and I never wanted to receive another call like the first one about Chad's white blood cell count. For the most part the news was good; the counts stayed down, and we borrowed time as we waited for what we hoped would be Chad's miracle drug, Gleevec.

During this time I continued my quest to draw closer to Christ, wanting every gift He could give me, as I explained to anybody who would listen. Few would. I'm sure they saw me as a father who couldn't deal with his son's illness and was compensating by becoming a religious fanatic. But couldn't many of the men of God in the Scriptures be described this way? John the Baptist wasn't anybody's idea of normal. I kept looking for people who believed God's power to heal through prayer was as available today as in biblical times.

I found one class of Christians who generally acknowledged the reality of miracles in the present day more readily: missionaries. I took to attending missionary conferences and talking with those who had been on the front lines of spiritual battles. I preferred those, as Isaiah says of the Messiah, who had "no form nor come-liness...no beauty that we should desire him" (Isa. 53:2 KJV). In fact, I sought out the least charismatic and, frankly, least attractive men and women of God at missionary conferences, the ones sit-ting alone in church halls behind folding tables waiting to speak to someone—anyone—about their ministries. I avoided mission-aries who naturally drew crowds, like the young evangelist who had recently spoken to tens of thousands in Sierra Leone or the vivacious blonde from Hong Kong with the hairdo of a TV anchor-woman. I wanted to know that God could bestow His power on *anybody*.

Dancing Through a Minefield

I found my man behind one of those folding tables at Maranatha Church, a corpulent fellow who ministered in what most would consider a godforsaken country, Zimbabwe—the site of recent presi-dential elections where the winner had to go into hiding from his outraged opponent. When I walked up to this missionary's table, he asked me, unused to the attention, "What are you doing here?"

"Have you seen miracles?"

His whole countenance changed. "Yes, I have."

"Are they real?"

"They are real. What's your name?"

I introduced myself.

"I can tell you a lot of stories, Dr. Crandall," he said.

"Tell me the most profound one."

He said, "Dr. Crandall, the power of God fell on our service one night. The power of God was so heavy, Dr. Crandall."

"What happened?"

He said, "We were in the small church—no more than a single room—we use for services, and there was only one lightbulb in the middle, hanging by a wire. I had the Word of God open and I was preaching, and the power of the Holy Spirit came on that room, and people started weeping, and it was like a thick cloud of the Holy Ghost filled the room—the Shechinah glory. As I walked about preaching, my shadow would fall on people from that one single light and they would be slain in the Spirit. They would collapse into a peaceful rest—the peace that passes all understanding."

"Really? You aren't exaggerating?"

He said, "Dr. Crandall, it was so powerful that my shadow would touch people, and just my shadow holding the Bible, the Word of God, would cover someone and the Holy Spirit would touch them."

"Anything else?"

"Well, what you have to understand is that the church was in the middle of a minefield. You can only get to it on a path that's been cleared. The mines left from previous wars have been marked but not all. It's still dangerous. We don't go into certain fields. But the Spirit of God hit us that night, and we were so full of joy, and the power of God was on us, and we started singing and dancing. We went out the door and started dancing in those fields, through the minefields, not knowing where we were going, but everyone came back safely. We danced through the minefields without one explosion."

I didn't quite know what to make of the minefield part of the story, although I certainly felt as if I were trying to dance through a minefield of my own. But the missionary's shadow having such a powerful effect was right in line with something that happened in the New Testament's book of Acts, where the people brought their sick out into the street so the apostle Peter's shadow could pass over them. "And all of them were healed," the book of Acts tells us (Acts 5:16). This man wasn't one to compare himself to Peter, and I had to think the similarity of the two phenomena was God-inspired. If it was true, the experience was certainly evidence that the power of God was as active today as in New Testament times, which was underlined by the similarity of the events taking place two thousand years apart.

I went home and told Deborah the missionary's story. "Miracles are happening, Deborah. Happening *today*. I know many of the people around us don't believe it, but I'm meeting men and women of God who do—people who have put their lives on the line. Why would they do that if it's not true?

"Chad can be cured if we cry out in Jesus' name!" I exclaimed. "I'm really starting to believe that. I don't quite know how to do it yet—or whether I have sufficient faith. I'm not sure that we can do this right by ourselves, but I'm searching for what God requires of us. I'm searching for God's power in healing Chad."

A lull in developments followed, as happens so many times in the spiritual life. And with it, discouragement, doubts about what I'd heard, suspicions that I was, as many of my friends concluded, resorting to religious fanaticism out of desperation. Three months later, I was almost out of hope. We had not found a way to obtain Gleevec for Chad. We didn't have anyone around us, really, who believed that Chad could be healed through prayer. Or at least it seemed that way, although I know our friends were praying for us—I just didn't get the sense that they thought their prayers would work; or I didn't believe enough myself that they would. That's the way discouragement works: it makes everything seem impossible.

A Man of God

One afternoon, very down, I told Deborah, "I just can't find any more people that believe."

She said, "There's a man of God who is coming to speak not far away in the town of Jupiter, and maybe he'll give you the answers or the inspiration or whatever it is you need—we need."

"A *man of God?*" The phrase struck me as hokey. "I don't know. No one *believes* anymore."

Discouraged as I was, I still agreed to attend the meeting, which took place after-hours at a private elementary school. I was on call that day, as it happened, in charge of all the heart attacks coming in—and were they ever coming in! It was the craziest day. It was like a battle in the heavens was being waged. Medevac helicopters arrived almost hourly with heart attack victims, and more came via ambulance. I spent all day and into the early evening ushering patients into operating rooms, supervising their treatment. One right after another.

The meeting was to start at 7:00 p.m. That hour came and went and I was still in the midst of caring for patients. "Lord, I need a break," I started praying. "I'm worn out and I'd like to get to this meeting. I promised Deborah, after all."

At around nine the new arrivals finally stopped. I jumped into my car still in my scrubs and headed north to Jupiter.

When I walked into the school I was glad to see the meeting was still in progress. Up front I saw the "man of God" for the first time, the missionary David Hogan. He looked like an older John the Baptist, if John the Baptist had worn country-and-western gear. He was tall and strong—an ox of a man. He wore a cowboy shirt with pearl buttons, blue jeans, a big ol' cowboy belt buckle, and sand-colored alligator-skin boots. He had a shock of white, coarse hair combed back from his forehead, a mustache and blunt-cut beard framing his mouth, and big, bottle-rim glasses behind which his eyes danced.

His preaching consisted of going through the Bible and its stories of healing, which he expanded by telling of miracles he had witnessed. He was detailing everything I had been studying, and he was grounded, orthodox, in his interpretations. I was impressed and attracted and at the same time overwhelmed.

The service was over before I knew it. I remained dumbstruck in my chair as people lined up for David Hogan to pray for them. Soon they started passing out in front of him—"slain in the Spirit." I knew what that was, although I had never seen it before. Never, ever, and it freaked me out. I looked more closely at the people lying on the floor, and their eyes were rolled back in their heads. I had to get out of there. This was too much. I was a Presbyterian! A doctor. Not someone to be hoodwinked through mass hypnosis by a backwoods evangelist dressed for a Grand Ole Opry audition.

I rose to leave, and all of a sudden I heard the Lord speak to me. I heard an actual voice: "Stay, this is for your son."

So I sat down. I thought I'd sit and watch. Hogan kept praying for people, many being slain in the Spirit. The more this happened, the greater his boldness in prayer. He spoke to people's conditions and prayed about their needs as someone called by God to do so, someone with authority. As the line shortened, I thought I'd have him pray for Chad. I was there, after all. What did I care what it looked like? Or who I was? What did any of that matter if Chad could be helped, in any way, by David Hogan's praying for him?

I walked up to the front and joined the line, four people in front of me, others behind. My legs started vibrating. I could barely stand up. I had no idea what was happening. I started going through a differential diagnosis, applying the criteria I knew as a physician. What might be causing my legs to shake? Was I nervous? Suffering from anxiety or stage fright? Might I be having a stroke? Could it be a pinched nerve? Why was this happening? What was going on? Every time I took a step I felt that my legs might collapse like those of a newborn calf.

Finally, I arrived at the front of the line. David Hogan held his hands out over my head, palms down. "What can I pray for you?" he asked.

"David, my son Chad has leukemia, and I can't find anyone to pray with who *really* believes that he can be healed. Will you pray for him?"

He said, "Absolutely." He started praying.

I figured I'd bow my head—that's what you do. As he prayed, I thought, *I've never heard anybody pray with this authority, this determination, or this boldness.*

I opened my eyes and looked at his face. It was blanched white. A scene flashed in my mind. We were in WWI and David was in a trench with all his weapons. He was climbing up the trench, and the enemy was on the other side. The enemy was coming forward, charging. The enemy in this visionary flash was Satan. He was coming toward us. David was face-to-face with the enemy and I could see his determination to take him out. That's what he looked like. He was battling for the life of my son!

Then, in a loud voice David Hogan said, "In the name of Jesus, Chad be healed!"

The next instant, I saw the tips of my feet up in the air as I was blown backward, landing about fifteen feet from where I had been standing. I landed on my back, unharmed, and in fact alert. I looked back toward David Hogan, wondering, *What happened? Did you see what happened? How did I get here?*

David Hogan wasn't fazed. He just went on and prayed for the next person who stepped up.

For a few more moments I sat on the floor, wondering what had happened. I hadn't been "slain in the Spirit" like the others—not exactly. I was far from enjoying a peaceful rest, which is how most people slain in the Spirit describe it. I felt weak—I could barely move—and again, strangely alert. I crawled over to a chair, where a little old lady was sitting, and as I pulled myself up and got back on my feet I asked her, "What happened?"

She said, "Doctor, don't ever forget this moment." I must have looked flabbergasted as she went on to explain. "You've been touched by the Holy Spirit."

"I have?"

"Yes, you have."

CHAPTER 5

"I Need Everything Jesus Can Give Me"

When I returned home that night, Deborah and I stayed up into the early morning hours discussing what had happened. I was always more skeptical of the supernatural than Deborah, and she readily accepted my being touched by the Holy Spirit.

What came about in my life as a result of the Holy Spirit's touch was as unexpected as the event itself, if less spectacular. I received a new boldness in pursuing the things of God—a release of spiritual enthusiasm. I couldn't wait to discover what other gifts God might bestow, and I wanted to be as faithful as possible—to show up for any divine appointments that might be in the offing—whatever that demanded, and however it might look. As a Christian, I was becoming radicalized.

As a family we began to attend a storefront Pentecostal church. There, the people with whom we were worshiping were in touch with their desperate need for Jesus, just as my family and I were. We knew how lost we would be without Him. There's a strange privilege in being desperate—one missing or not felt so immediately in most conventional church circles. It's why the tax collectors and prostitutes of Jesus' day recognized Him so much more easily as their champion than did the religious authorities.

Not just once but every week we gathered at that church and prayed for Chad's healing.

One of the elders of the church had been miraculously healed of a back injury. Chad, with his childlike faith, was particularly eager for this elder to pray for him. The elder asked Chad if there was any unforgiveness in his heart.

Chad turned and asked, "Mom, do I have unforgiveness?"

The elder explained how to release these negative feelings to God. After praying Chad was satisfied he had done so. Then the elder began to pray.

As the elder prayed Chad felt cold air rush out his fingertips and by the time he got home and began getting ready for bed, he said, "I'm not heavy anymore; I feel so light. I used to feel like I had a thousand pounds strapped to my back. But it's gone!"

By the late fall of 2000, with prayer times like this and initial treatment, we learned that Chad's leukemia had unexpectedly regressed from the acute phase back to the chronic phase—the presence of the disease was so minimal it showed up only in blood tests. Miraculously, Chad regained much of the weight he had lost, his muscle tone improved, and the color even came back into his cheeks. We were elated, of course. Particularly as this gave us more time for Gleevec to come on the market.

Mexico: The Blind See, the Lame Walk

About three months after I was touched by the Holy Spirit—or more accurately, blown back (and away) by the Holy Ghost—I called the missionary David Hogan and voiced my heart's desire. "I am fighting for the life of my son, and I need everything Jesus can give me."

He said, "If you truly want the living Christ and all He can give you—as well as demand from you, because God is a jealous God, Dr. Crandall—why don't you fly down to our mission post in Mexico?"

I wouldn't be joining David Hogan there but one of his missionary associates, Greg Rider. At first I was disappointed, but David reminded me that I was taking this trip to encounter Jesus in a new way, not to get caught up in hero worship. I saw his point. This made me think even more highly of Hogan's spiritual maturity.

So I flew down to the Gulf Coast of Mexico, landing in the shoreline city of Tampico. Eastern Mexico is a vast alluvial plain that declines steeply from the continental ridge bisecting the country. In this part of Mexico the climate gradually turns from subtropical to tropical. To the west of Tampico, where I would be staying for the next three weeks, the land is hilly and then mountainous, cut up into a maze of small farms and villages. Sagebrush and Joshua trees carpet the landscape as in a high desert, although there are isolated stands of pine. The land suffers from deforestation because the people have used most of the trees for their shacks and cooking.

My plane landed late at night. Greg Rider was there to meet me in his small Japanese pickup. I'm not sure what I was thinking about the conditions I'd find, but I was dressed in regulation Palm Beach traveling attire: blue blazer, open-collared white shirt, khaki pants, tasseled loafers. Greg told me to throw my suitcase in the flatbed and hop in after it. The cab was filled with Greg's Mexican coworkers.

I tried not to complain that this was no way to treat a guest, but as we drove into the mountains for the next three hours, I was jounced and rattled and thumped within an inch of my life. Eastern Mexico was experiencing a cold snap, and I couldn't wrap my blue blazer tight enough. I got the intended message big-time that I was not going to be treated as anything special.

When we arrived at Greg's house at nearly 3:00 a.m., all the lights were blazing, and his whole family—his wife and children and people I would come to know as part of his missionary team— met us at the door.

"Do they always meet you like this?" I asked. I couldn't believe they had all waited up for him.

He said, "Dr. Crandall, we've lost eleven missionaries. They've been killed preaching the Word of God. When I return home, my family honors me by greeting me at the front door, whatever time it is. They know that one day I might not come back."

Once inside, after hugs and handshakes, Greg turned to me and said, "I know why you're here, Dr. Crandall. You want to meet Jesus. The Jesus you've never met. The Jesus you've never known. You're going to. Starting at 7:00 a.m. Can you get up by then?"

"I'm a doctor," I said. "I'm used to being on call at all hours."

"We start the day by reading the Word of God," he said. "You'll see. I bet you'll like it."

The next morning at seven, Greg and his extended family gathered and read from the Bible: portions of the Old Testament,

Psalms, Proverbs, and the New Testament. Greg read and his wife read, as did his children and members of his missionary team. They even passed the Bible my way. Then for a half hour we sang praise songs to cassette tape accompaniment.

"Now let's go out and preach the gospel!" Greg exclaimed.

David Hogan and his associates' ministry on Mexico's Gulf Coast is directed toward indigenous tribes—the groups of people the Spanish found when Hernán Cortés and other explorers came to the New World early in the sixteenth century. Even more than Native Americans, these Mexican tribal peoples remain distinct from the larger society, with their own dialects and customs. Many practice tribal religions or combine pagan beliefs with an untutored Catholicism, compromising the genuine message. After five centuries these tribal peoples have hardly been evangelized.

Greg and I and another truckload of coworkers drove out to a village, an outpost of a dozen families in wood shacks. Those better off had corrugated iron roofs; the poorer, thatch. An open sewer ran through the village's "Main Street." Flea-bitten dogs poked their noses at us and chickens scratched and strutted. This was very much the third world.

Two or three dozen villagers began arriving, nevertheless, to the preformed concrete brick building they used as a Protestant church. A few of Greg's coworkers were musicians, and they started the singing of praise songs with a mariachi bounce. I noticed that the people were wearing what must have been their Sunday best, checked shirts and clean dungarees for the men, long skirts with ruffled fringes for the ladies. Everyone sang his or her heart out. The people sang in their dialect, which I didn't understand, but it was beautiful. I started to feel that God had arrived.

Greg opened his Bible, read a passage, and began preaching.

His preparation consisted of mainly constant prayer and constant Bible reading, which gave him the confidence to rely on God's inspiration when the time came for him to preach. He didn't have four points and three illustrations, as conventional sermons go. His sermons were free-form elaborations on biblical texts as these applied to the people. As his heart longed for God's own and beat with the people's, his sermons always proved to be as deep and clear as the biblical text and conveyed their inspiration by the Holy Spirit. As my designated translator, one of Greg's sons, whispered into my ear, I was shocked that anyone speaking off-the-cuff could be so eloquent.

At the end of the service, the sick came forward for healing prayer. The deaf, the blind, the mute, the lame, those suffering from debilitating illness, machete wounds, and complaints only they could know. It was a scene right out of the New Testament. One woman who had been crippled for years was transported from her mountaintop farm to the meeting in a wheelbarrow. Her care-givers—rather rudely, I thought—dumped her out before Greg on the floor. With Bible in hand, Greg and another local minister prayed over her. She got up on her feet and walked out!

I didn't know the details of her condition, of course, and couldn't help but be curious, but I saw her walk out with my own eyes and I doubt she would have been delivered in a wheelbarrow if she hadn't been a cripple. I was amazed.

That same day Greg Rider and his team conducted midday and afternoon services, and each time Greg would open to a fresh passage of Scripture and begin speaking as the Spirit moved him. I found the way in which the sick came to the services extremely moving, as they presented themselves with a quiet dignity, willing, hopeful, never presumptuous, but waiting on God with true faith.

Medical Science and God's Healing

I was more prone to jump to conclusions or to become so enthusiastic that I could become cocksure as to how God would act. In the late afternoon of the first day an accident occurred that bewildered me and eventually served as a helpful caution. While riding his motocross bike to a meeting, one of the missionaries was struck by a bus. He was transported in the back of a pickup to Greg Rider's house, where the team was having its evening meal.

They put him on the kitchen table, and I could see that his arm was distorted—he had one or more simple fractures, and his shoulder was badly dislocated. Even though he was screaming in pain, I could only think: *I can't wait to see everyone pray over this man and his arm be restored!* The hair on the back of my hands was standing up. We were going to see a miracle right there and then! "Oh, Jesus, thank You!" The team would pray and that shoulder would go right back into its joint. I had what God should do all planned out for God.

Then Greg Rider looked at me and asked, "What do you think we should do, Doc?"

"Let's get to praying for him!"

"Dr. Crandall," he said, "you have to fix his arm."

The man was still screaming, but I was starting to feel angry. "I'm not touching his arm! I came from the States to see miracles, and I am not touching his arm. You're men of God. You need to pray for him."

They did and nothing happened. The poor man was helpless with misery.

Greg renewed his request. "Doc, you have to help him. You need to fix his arm *now.*"

I could hardly get over my disappointment enough to act, but I jumped up and stood on the table, took the man's arm, and put my foot in his armpit for leverage. "Now everyone pray in the name of Jesus!" I ordered. I pulled and popped the arm right back into joint, straightening the fractures in the process.

I remained disappointed, though. I was so eager to see the supernatural at that point that I couldn't distinguish calling upon God from presuming the actions of God. Later, wise teachers like Reinhard Bonnke helped me think through the difference. My skills as a physician were, after all, a gift that God had already supplied. Nothing was necessary to the man's healing other than my acting on what I knew very well how to do. Who was I to order God around as to the method of the man's healing?

God created the natural order—the way this world works—and most often works through it in order to accomplish God's ends. He intervenes in the natural order or redirects that order most often, I've come to believe, when only God's intervention will suffice and usually when His miraculous power will teach us about His ultimate purpose—the defeat of death itself and the restoration of all things in God's eternal kingdom. At the time I didn't understand these things.

A Modern-Day Stoning

Soon enough, though, Greg, his team, and I were in a situation where God's direct intervention was necessary and instructive.

Greg Rider and his team were holding a meeting in a village after nightfall. We were gathered in an open field, around a Coleman lantern. There were only about a dozen in attendance. Greg had been preaching for some minutes when I heard a thud, and then another and another. Something skipped by in the grass. I saw people ducking and covering their heads. Stones were raining down on us.

I looked at Greg. "What's going on?"

"You've heard about people being stoned in the Bible? There's a group that doesn't like it when we come to this village, and they are trying to drive us off."

He then addressed the whole meeting in a firm voice. "Everyone, let's pray that no one gets hurt. We are going to finish the meeting. We will not leave. We will not run. We will not take cover. We will call on almighty God that none of us will be injured or hurt.

"In the mighty name of Jesus," Greg cried, "I ask You, God, that no one be injured or hurt, no one be stoned in this meeting this night. Shield us from the stones, Lord. Deflect the stones. Cover us with Your protective hand."

Greg Rider stopped praying and started preaching again, but the stones kept coming. They were being thrown from the surrounding woods that hid our attackers. The stones became larger—more lethal. The rocks were so big, finally, that they were like shot puts. People were hurling them with all their might.

We did not move, although I was tempted to run, I can tell you.

The rocks at last stopped coming and no one had been hurt. I thought back to Greg's family's greeting him at three o'clock in the morning and understood much more immediately why.

When we returned to his house, I said to Greg, "Your God can do this?"

He said, "Oh yeah, Dr. Crandall, when we call on the name of Jesus, and we really need Him, He answers us. We have no one else here but Jesus to protect us. We don't have a police force. In situations like that, we have nothing but the power of God, and we have learned to rely on God's power."

"But when you have a doctor, you use a doctor," I said, teasing him.

"Sure, why wouldn't we?"

A Burden for Souls

For more than two weeks I went to meeting after meeting with Greg Rider and his team. I'll never forget piling into the back of his pickup truck one day and driving for fourteen hours to a village. Fourteen hours—one way—over dirt roads that were rutted and potholed. That drive left my entire body aching. My back hurt, my kidneys hurt, my arms and legs were sore and bruised; I had such a headache from being the jack-in-the-box that my eyes felt ready to pop. Once we finally stopped, I wondered aloud to Greg why we had come all this way.

"For two people," he said.

"Two?" I was incredulous.

"I was here on my dirt bike a while ago. The two we're here for said they'd become Christians if I came back. Isn't it great? There'll be rejoicing in heaven tonight!"

The two villagers came to worship and pray with us, and they did accept Jesus Christ as Savior.

I saw something in Greg then that was even greater than his gifts of preaching and healing—a burden for souls, the desire to see people enter God's kingdom. We all want to know God is there and loves us and is willing to meet our needs, particularly in difficult circumstances. We rejoice easily in the spectacular phenomena of supernatural healing; miracles part the curtains and we are given a privileged glimpse into eternity. One that's pretty obvious, for someone with any faith at all.

Rejoicing over conversions is a different story. Although most Christians say that they are inspired by conversions, few of us are as enthusiastic about people being received into the kingdom as we are about supernatural healings. That day in Mexico I had to ask myself whether I really believed enough in the importance of evangelism that I would have volunteered to take the trip if I had known in advance how arduous it would prove to be. But as I witnessed those two people's accepting Christ, one old man and one old woman, kneeling in the dirt with clasped hands, confessing Christ as their Savior and Lord, I understood, even if I still didn't get as pumped up, that this miracle was even more important than a supernatural healing, because it was the healing of these souls for eternity. They were being rescued from eternal separation from God to enjoy His company endlessly, in both this life and the world to come.

The fourteen hours back weren't short, but they were eased by what Christ had accomplished through Greg's faithfulness and even my part in being along for the ride.

One of the important experiences of being with Greg Rider and his team in Mexico consisted in their relating the many miracles they had witnessed. Over meals, on our forays out in the trucks, Greg and his team told of healing after healing. They had witnessed many other miracles like the wheelbarrow woman's regaining the ability to walk and God's protection on the night it rained rocks. They weren't building themselves up with mere wishful thinking, either. Nothing like that could have kept them going, because their life was hard, dangerous, and isolating. They spoke of what they had seen with an awe that truly made them consider the life they led privileged. A type of privilege about as far from the privileges of Palm Beach as can be imagined.

The Principle of Exchange

When I returned home, I gave Deborah a prayer cloth that I had taken to every healing service along the journey. It was a simple red-and-black bandanna. I didn't tell her what it was, but when she held it in her hands, she almost fainted away. She took a couple of steps backward and said, "*Wooooo.* What is *that?*" I explained how many times it had been blessed and prayed over, following the biblical precedent in Acts 19:11–12, where handkerchiefs and aprons that had touched the apostle Paul were taken to the sick and their diseases healed.

In my absence God had performed another work of healing, as Chad was visibly improved. He had begun to grow again!

This was a first instance of a deep spiritual principle that I would come to recognize more and more—the principle of exchange. There are countless instances and varieties of exchange in the spiritual life. For example, Jesus asks us to forgive others as God forgives us. He pledges that God will extend mercy to the merciful. The most fundamental exchange consists in Jesus' promise that if we will give Him our lives, He will give us life in abundance—His eternal life. And, He says, what you have done for the "least of these my brethren"—His followers who are poor, without resources, in trouble—you "have done it unto me" (Matt. 25:40 KJV). *God blesses us when we allow ourselves to be used by God to bless others.* So while I was helping out with the work of God in Mexico, God was blessing our family through improving Chad's health. I would keep encountering this principle of exchange as I grew in my spiritual life.

After I related to Deborah some of what had happened in Mexico, I said, "Our Lord is real. We will make it through this."

"I know we will," she said.

"I've seen Him, Deborah. I've felt Him. It's different now. I know that He's real." That night Deborah and I went to the boys' bedroom. They slept in bunk beds, Chad on the top. Deborah and I began praying for him, pouring out our hearts, praising God for all He had done for Chad and asking Him to continue to bless him. Our prayers turned into a vigil, as we stayed with the boys for the next three hours, adoring God's greatness, extolling His majesty, thanking God for His generosity.

"Where Are My Indians?"

As I've indicated before, spiritual enthusiasm waxes and wanes. About three months after my return from Mexico, I became discouraged once more. This time I didn't doubt what I had seen in Mexico. I was simply all too aware of what a contrast it made to my life in Palm Beach. Everywhere Greg and his fellow missionaries went the favor of God was on them. The villagers, as poor as they were, were glad to hear of God's love for them and responded with open hearts. In contrast, so many in my world seemed completely indifferent to God's love, if not actively in rebellion against it. They found God's reaching out to them an affront to their dignity.

I actually began thinking about leaving medicine altogether and becoming a missionary. I felt the urge to pack up the whole family and move to our own Gulf Coast Mexican hacienda.

I talked to Deborah one night about this. "No one gets excited about Jesus in Palm Beach," I said. "Our neighbors have all the money, the fame. They don't want Jesus, Deborah. But I do. And I want my Indians, Deborah. I want to minister to people, proclaiming the name of Jesus. People who will be receptive."

In my private prayers, I kept crying out to God, "Where are my Indians? Where are the people to whom I have been called? Who wants to hear the Word of God and will rejoice in it?"

One morning about seven thirty I was on the bottom floor of Good Samaritan Hospital where the morgue is located. Most of the lights were out and I was standing in the shadows, waiting for the elevator. I pushed the button several times to go up. The thought that had been nagging me came up once more. *Where are my Indians, Lord? I need my Indians, because I can't keep going on without my people group. You need to identify who they are, where I need to go, what I need to do.* I hit the button again. *Where are my Indians?*

All of a sudden the Lord spoke to me. I heard an audible voice. I've heard the Lord speak audibly only a few times. The Lord said, "Your Indians are your patients. I've given them to you, and I haven't given them to anyone else. If you don't get them saved, no one else will. If you don't get them healed, no one else will. I've given them to you."

That was a total revelation in my life—and eventually made for revolutionary changes in my medical practice.

I took off like a rocket that morning, praying all day long. "Lord, You've given me these patients? You've given me these people, here? They say they don't want You, but You've given them to me? And now they're mine, and if I don't witness to them, they won't receive Jesus?

"I don't have to leave medicine? I don't have to go someplace else? You've given me these people?"

What really woke me up was that He said, "If you don't get them saved, no one else will." That rocked me. It changed my whole outlook on ministry, on life.

I instantly became comfortable with what I was doing, where I was. All I had to do was work within the medical system with my patients, and within my own community. My Indians were the people around me; the people I worked with every day. (Now when I speak to churches and other audiences, I make a point of how we've all been given the people around us, at work, in our offices, and neighborhoods. We are all where we are for a reason.) I might have known this all along, of course, but hearing God's voice finally convinced me to open my eyes and see the tremendous need of people around me.

Praying for My Patients

Several months before Chad became sick I had thought of praying for my patients and began doing so in a general way. But now I knew I had to pray for them specifically and in their presence, if they consented. I promised the Lord I would pray aloud for one person a week and asked Him to lead me to the right person. I wondered whether the principle of exchange would continue to apply. If I prayed for my patients, would my own family be blessed— would Chad continue to improve?

While I had made the resolution to pray aloud for at least one patient a week, I was nervous and embarrassed and put it off. At the end of the first week I told myself that I absolutely must pray for one patient that very day. Still, I waited until the very last patient of the day. I figured if she became upset, no one else would be in the office and there wouldn't be a scene.

My last patient was a woman in her eighties who had enjoyed a celebrated career in the New York fashion world. Mrs. Green had some heart issues; nothing terribly serious. She was still an attractive woman with thick silver hair brushed back behind her ears, large, deep-set eyes, and a slim, erect carriage. She was soft-spoken but direct—a woman who had taken care of herself for many years and still could. She was my last opportunity, if I was going to carry through with my commitment.

I finally asked, "Do you mind if I pray for you? I'd like to. Would you mind?"

"Oh, no; you can pray for me," she said. She seemed truly grateful to be asked.

I took her hand and I said, "Father God, in the name of Jesus, I pray for Mrs. Green. I pray that she will be well, Father, and I pray blessings over her, in the name of Jesus."

That's all I prayed.

She started crying.

I thought, *Oh, no! I've offended her. I've hurt her in some way. What's happened?*

"Mrs. Green, are you okay?" I handed her a tissue.

She said, "Oh, Dr. Crandall, I'm fine."

"Then why are you crying? Is something wrong?"

"You don't understand," she said. "No one has prayed for me for forty years. That was so nice. It was like I felt the hand of God on me when you prayed. Thank you. Thank you for praying for me."

After she left the office, I was tremendously pumped. *Who's next?* Where was the next patient? I couldn't wait to do it again!

A couple of weeks later, I was in my office when I received a phone call from the emergency room. They had a patient with severe headaches.

"Why are you calling me? I'm a heart doctor, not a headache doctor. Call his primary care physician."

"He doesn't have one. We just need someone to take a look and we thought you might."

"Okay, get a CT scan of his brain. Let me know what you find and I'll do what I can."

I was still working in my office when the emergency room physician called back. "He has brain tumors," he said. "Multiple brain tumors. It doesn't look good."

I asked that a chest X-ray be taken, since lung cancer often spreads to the brain. Sadly, I guessed right.

"What do you want us to do?" the emergency room doctor asked once more.

"Get the neurologist and the oncologist. I'll come down and talk with him."

The patient was a relatively young man. I wondered what I could offer him; by the time lung cancer spreads to the brain there's usually little that can be done.

The patient's name was Richard, and when I met him in the emergency room he was smiling. He asked for my recommendation. "It doesn't look good, does it, Doctor?" he asked. He was trying his best to remain good-humored, even to the point of being kind to his doctor. I immediately felt tremendous sympathy for this man.

"I'm sorry," I said, "it doesn't. I'm going to get you the best doctor I can, though. Let's see if we can beat this thing." Then I added, "But you know, Richard, I've been reading my Bible, and it says in my Bible that we can pray for the sick. Would you mind if I just prayed for you?"

He said, "Sure, pray; do it."

He was on the examination table, sitting up. I went to the right side and took his hand. I prayed, "Father God, I ask that You heal Richard of his brain tumors and his lung tumors, and I ask this in the name of Jesus. Amen."

Once again, I didn't say much in my prayer, but I've found it doesn't take much; God only wants to know what we are asking of Him. Our prayers are like a laser signal to heaven for God to enter the scene.

Then I said, "Richard, I've done everything I can do. I've prayed for you. The Bible commands me to do that. I don't understand why supernatural healing comes about sometimes, but I know we can always ask the Lord for it and we should do so *believing* the Lord can heal. So I'm going to get the best doctors and I'm going to *believe* that you will be healed."

I did get Richard the best doctors I could, but I have to admit that my belief in his supernatural healing was fleeting. When I walked out of the room, I couldn't suppress the conviction that his life would soon be over.

Six months went by. My nurse came running into the office one day. "Hey," she said, "Richard's back."

I was surprised he'd lasted this long. I could only imagine that he must look eaten up with cancer. "What does he look like?" I asked, not really wanting to hear her answer.

"He looks pretty good," she said brightly. "You have to see this."

So I walked into the examination room where he was waiting. He did look good. Really good. In fact, he looked *great*. "Richard, what's going on? What happened?"

"Don't you remember?"

"Remember what?" I couldn't suppress the thought—*he should be dead!*

"Don't you remember that day you came into the ER and prayed for me? I went to the doctors, and they gave me minimal treatment, and all those brain tumors and lung tumors disappeared. They call it a miracle."

After Richard (and how happy I was about Richard!), instead of praying for one patient a week, I began to pray for one patient a day and then more than one a day. I told myself, *If I can pray for my son, I can pray for my patients. And maybe, if I keep praying for my patients, there'll be an exchange, because someone will start praying for my son and he'll get well, too.*

I was *pumped*. I started putting Bibles in all my exam rooms— gospel tracts, too. I began praying for about half my patients every day. It got so out of control that my office always ran overtime.

CHAPTER 6

The Perfect Couple?

Not quite a year after Chad's diagnosis, in May 2001, I received a call from Novartis Pharmaceuticals with the news we had been praying for: Gleevec had been approved by the FDA for the treatment of CML and would be available by the end of the month. Within four days of Chad's beginning to take the medication, his blood counts were normal, his leukemia undetectable. As Dr. Brian Druker in Oregon had forecast, Gleevec stopped the disease dead in its tracks.

We were grateful for this, on many levels! Prior treatment and prayer had controlled Chad's leukemia but allowed for the possibility of new strains developing. Once another line of stem cells goes bad by virtue of slight mutations, the progress of the disease becomes almost impossible to stop. It metastasizes, producing tumors in different parts of the body. Chad had been healthy enough the last nine months to attend school, play tennis, and live the life of any other eleven- to twelve-year-old. I thought, *Now he might live a long life, with his CML in remission for years to come!*

When I think of that happy time I remember especially the summer's highlight: the finals of the Palm Beach Bath & Tennis Club's junior championship. Once Chad started playing tennis seriously, he started dreaming of winning our club's junior championship. The winner's name is added to a plaque celebrating the club's past champions, with the list going back generations. That roll call was Chad's Hall of Fame.

Going into the championship, Chad was playing his best tennis and was expected to do well. But the club has many fine young players who receive instruction from former touring professionals. The club's juniors always include a number of players with high rankings in the state of Florida. In a place like Palm Beach achievement isn't virtually a religion; *it's far more important than that.* You can imagine the lengths to which many parents, with money to burn, go in forwarding their children's tennis careers.

Deborah and I didn't have to work all that hard with our boys, since Chad would recruit his brother into marathon all-day sessions and, failing this, would beat a ball against a backboard for hours at a time. Still, we knew he would face stiff competition.

What we did not know was that his brother, Christian, would make one of the runs of his life through the draw. In the semifinals he met a boy who was among those favored to win the entire championship and Christian pulled off a huge upset. This meant Chad and Christian would face each other in the finals.

For most parents, I would suppose, this would be an occasion of anxiety. Whom to root for? How to celebrate the winner while simultaneously consoling the loser?

Deborah and I felt the conflict, but, honestly, as we sat at a parasol table by the feature court, watching our boys trying to beat each other, we enjoyed the perspective we had gained during the previous months. Towheaded Chad, with his consistent groundies and scurrying defense, versus taller, dark-haired Christian with his bombing serve and killer forehand: they were such complements, even on the tennis court! And they were both healthy, vital, full of life. I could have watched that match until the end of time. How I loved my boys.

At a changeover, I remember taking Deborah's hand and exchanging a look illuminated by our life together—a look that expressed our oneness. Through the years we have truly become each other's life.

I suppose to an outside observer we must have looked at that moment like the perfect cinematic family. For one thing, Deborah is quite beautiful, a woman who might have stepped out of a Ralph Lauren catalog. And there I was, Yale-educated, a former university professor and now a cardiologist in a community that controls 25 percent of the wealth in the entire country. At a prestigious club. Watching our boys play for the junior championship. What could be more palmy?

Knowing about Chad's illness changed the picture, but there was much more. The look Deborah and I shared recalled a challenging history that was anything but celluloid perfect. *"I will find a way"* had been my motto, in part because doing so had been such an enormous struggle. In making our life together, we had overcome family history, early mistakes, spiritual naïveté, and the world's resistance to our hopes and dreams. We had fought not only against flesh and blood, as the apostle Paul wrote, but against principalities and powers and the rulers of the air. We had come along far enough, at this point, for "I will find a way" to be replaced with "God, please show us the way."

Leukemia wasn't the first evil we had encountered. As I mentioned, we thought we might never have children and prayed for ten years before seeing our sons born.

I didn't exactly sail into the medical profession, either, and while I was struggling to become a doctor, Deborah confronted her own health struggles.

So what we felt at that moment—watching our boys battle it out on the court—wasn't so much triumph as being brought into a period of rest. Deborah and I had been through too much to imagine we had just "arrived," as we foolishly once might have.

The Girl of My Dreams

I have to admit, though, that we started out in life as the ideal high school couple. Not exactly the high school quarterback and the head cheerleader, but close. I played middle linebacker and was named All-State. Deborah could have been a star athlete herself; however, she was interested not in sports but fashion, as she told the coaches who were always trying to recruit her. She did some modeling and could have made it her career but decided otherwise. We were voted the "best dressed" couple of our senior class.

It was love at first sight—at least for me. I saw her at a high school football game and instantly told my friend, "That's the girl I'm going to marry." She had piercing blue eyes. She was tall, five feet, seven inches, and thin, with long blond hair that draped over her shoulders and down her back. She was fair-complexioned but tanned in a way that highlighted her coloring. The girl of my dreams.

From that moment I began pursuing her relentlessly, with all the charm a sixteen-year-old boy could muster. I had more energy than I knew what to do with and worked every odd job I could find so I always had cash, which I spent freely on Deborah, taking her out to nice restaurants and giving her small gifts such as records and turquoise earrings and leather bracelets. (Remember those?)

The social setting in which we grew up made finding our way confusing. Since we lived just outside Washington, D.C., in a suburb inhabited by high government officials—one of our neighbors was the CIA director—we came of age under the guidance of people who had achieved much in life. My father was a high-ranking military officer before he started a very successful real-estate development company. Deborah's dad managed the business side of Foundry United Methodist Church in D.C.

But the pleasure-seeking atmosphere of the late 1960s and early 1970s led me to put more emphasis on having fun and partying than attending to my studies. Somehow, though, I always felt I would attend medical school and become a doctor, and looking back, I see my aptitude for medicine was clear. My high school teacher for chemistry and biology noted I had a gift for these subjects and encouraged me to take them more seriously. Like many future scientists and doctors, I liked putting together collections and roamed the nearby woods collecting animal skeletons, insect specimens, and historical artifacts like old bottles, crockery, buttons, and the Civil War bullets that would pop up now and again.

Deborah and I graduated from high school in 1972. Deborah decided to attend college in Northern Virginia—she felt more comfortable staying home for the first couple of years before venturing out. The education offered at Northern Virginia was far superior to most state colleges, as PhDs who worked for governmental agencies like the State Department and the Centers for Disease Control served as adjunct faculty.

I Party, Deborah Prays

I went off to East Carolina University in Greenville, North Carolina, where I took eighteen credit hours in subjects including calculus, biochemistry, and biology while majoring in "Fraternity Party." I crashed and burned and had to come home after a disastrous first semester.

While I was away, Deborah made key decisions about her life's direction. Her brother had become a serious Christian and would in due course become a minister in the Evangelical Free Church. He was following his forebears in his choice of vocations, as Deborah's mother was the daughter of a Methodist minister and her family tree was full of pastors and missionaries. As Deborah began her college career, her brother asked her a troubling question: "If you died, do you know that you would go to heaven?" He spoke of a personal faith that went far beyond the moralism of the church in which they had grown up, which Deborah had rejected as too much and unnecessary.

The issue of Deborah's destiny beyond death would not leave her alone. She drove a white MG Midget and during much of her first semester in college she took drives by herself, thinking over the question. Driving the car made her feel as if she was getting somewhere even as she remained undecided. She began attending a Bible study at the college, where she met friends who attended the House of Bread at Truro Episcopal Church—a center of the charismatic renewal then taking place across denominations. The charismatic renewal emphasized gifts of the Holy Spirit such as supernatural healing and speaking in tongues. More and more of the people she met had the same type of "too intense" faith as her brother.

Deborah was very popular in high school, but she wasn't by any means a party girl. She did not like it when I drank too much. Since I could take it or leave it, I cut back for her sake. Dating her, I realized how frightened—terrified, really—she was of situations that threatened to spiral out of control. "If you ever hurt me, that's it!" she said. I had no reason to doubt her and never for a moment thought of jeopardizing our relationship—I knew from the beginning she would always be the most important human being in my life.

I found loving Deborah unconditionally as natural as breathing. Who wouldn't love her? She was fun, athletic, artistic, and her willowy beauty made me want to wrap my arms around her.

Deborah was also afraid God would ask of her things contrary to her nature. She thought a lot about the unfashionable wardrobe she might have to wear. This may sound trite, but Deborah was just discovering her substantial artistic gifts, which would lead her one day into a career in graphic design. No one wants to choose between being fully human—fully who he or she is—and belonging to God. We actually don't have to—God made us who we are, after all, and takes pleasure in the gifts, such as creativity, that He gives us. But that's the way the choice to become an "intense

Christian" seemed to Deborah at the time. Accepting God's invitation to have a relationship with God through Jesus Christ felt like giving up on the person she hoped to become.

Her Christian conversion came about quietly and unobtrusively. She was alone in her home one night, where she had been thinking all evening about praying in the way her brother had suggested, giving herself to God. By the time she had walked from her second-story bedroom down the stairs to the living room, she had surrendered herself completely to Christ.

When she walked onto the Northern Virginia Community College campus the next day she found she had a compassion for her fellow students she had never known before. *I've changed!* she thought, wondering at what had happened. "I'm starting to care about people," she told me a few days later. This came as a shock since I had always found her a loving person, not only toward me but her many friends as well. But think how much sense this makes as a sign of Deborah's encounter with God. When a child's relationship with a parent becomes unpredictable and troubling, the child naturally grows up wary and likely cold. This person also masters hiding his or her true feelings, wearing an encouraging smile even while edging toward the door. John's First Letter in the New Testament tells us that if we claim to love God but hate our brothers, we are liars. Deborah's newfound love for God opened her up to other people in a new way. God had brought about a substantial emotional healing that she had not even been looking for—likely healing she was not even aware she needed.

What Deborah experienced was so real that she began telling me I needed to know God in a whole new way. I thought I knew at least as much about Christianity as she did. My family attended a

Presbyterian church. I had earned my God and Country medal in the Boy Scouts! I was a Christian.

Not in the way I needed to be, she kept claiming.

This gradually introduced a rift between us. Just as she had let me know that I could never hurt her, she now informed me she would never marry me unless I came to know Jesus Christ as my Lord and Savior. She wanted me to be one of those born-again people. I went with her to the Truro church's House of Bread worship service, where people were raising their hands as they prayed and singing at the top of their lungs. As much as I loved Deborah, I didn't know if all that was for me. Perhaps it would turn out to be just one of her passing enthusiasms.

Worm Motel

I finally settled into my studies, at least in part, at Northern Virginia. I continued taking the basic sciences I would need for a premed major and I was also attracted to anthropology—the study of people groups and their cultures.

In 1974, the summer between my sophomore and junior years, I took a trip to West Africa in the company of my anthropology professor and two other students, to the nation of Togo, in order to study the Kabre tribe—a people who lived on the savannah north of the coast.

We arrived first at Lomé, the capital, which even today is a bare-bones city of rough-plastered, low-lying concrete buildings, gimcrack houses with metal roofs, and even more modest shops and bars that are little more than huts. Open sewers ran along the streets and there were more than a few beggars who lacked limbs. Lomé was a nightmarish introduction to the third world.

We had barely arrived when we found that our professor, a PhD who also worked as a State Department official, had taken off to enjoy one of the city's brothels. He had taken all our money as well, which we had entrusted to him for safekeeping. Toward evening my two fellow students and I found ourselves wandering the streets, asking people where we might sleep—cheaply. We couldn't afford any of the hotels in town, as bad as they were. Finally, we found what might be described as a Togo "motel," which consisted of a series of mud huts connected to one another like the body segments of a grub worm. My knapsack on my back, sleeping bag in hand, I was led through the connecting chambers of the worm to a room with a little bed. The bed was so disgusting, a breeding ground for bedbugs and lice, that I quickly abandoned the idea of sleeping there. But I had ten dollars in my pocket—that was it.

The other male student in the group, Chris Croff, was at my side. He had a good heart but a scary appearance; he had been in a car accident and had a scar that ran at a slashing angle from his right temple across his left cheek. He liked the intimidating way it made him look—he had refused plastic surgery—and right then so did I; I wanted to keep his menacing mug as close as possible. While we were sizing up the situation, prostitutes kept traipsing by leading customers by the hand. "I can't sleep here," I told Chris and motioned for him to follow me back the way we came.

We had first entered the worm motel through a larger room with a bamboo bar. The bar area was not being used and we found it deserted. "I'm sleeping here," I said and rolled out my sleeping bag on the floor. When I lay down the trouble we were in hit me. What if the good professor never came back with our tickets and money? The suffocating atmosphere of the place pressed down with ever more weight on my chest. I started to have an anxiety meltdown, sweat beading up on my forehead. If I needed medical attention, where would I go in what was now the middle of the night in Lomé? I didn't speak French, the language of the country. How would I communicate? I looked over at Chris, who had laid out his sleeping bag as well, and said, "I think I'm in trouble here. I don't know what I'm feeling, but it's not good."

I looked around and noticed a global map behind the bar—the continents spread out from left to right, the tip of Siberia showing at the extreme far left and once again at the extreme far right. The map had a severe tear right through the middle of the Atlantic Ocean, the Americas ruptured from Europe and Africa. Part of the tear flapped over the eastern seaboard of the United States. How was I ever going to get back there? I started weeping. I told Chris, "We are in trouble, man."

As we had tried to find a place to sleep, we had passed a voodoo fetish shop, where half-rotted dogs' heads rested in a grocer's bin like so many cabbages. In Togo death seemed to leer at you from every corner. Our professor had run off, we had no money, and we were sleeping in a prostitutes' den. I was in total culture shock and more scared than I had ever been in my life. My friend Chris, whom I thought to be a believer, kept this mostly to himself. At that moment I was willing to try anything. "Listen, man," I said to Chris, "we have to pray to get out of this."

I had never prayed in the way I did right then. I remember Deborah telling me, "If you ask the Lord into your life, you'll have peace." I cried out to God, "Father God, come into my life!" I started hearing Deborah's words again: "If you repent of your sins, He will forgive you, but you have to repent of your sins and ask

Him into your life." "Yes, Lord," I said, "I repent of my sins and I ask You to forgive me. I ask You into my heart and life and I am sorry, Lord, that I have sinned and been a sinner." I prayed right out loud, and my friend with the scar on his face was looking at me as if I were the oddest thing he had seen in Togo. There I was, on my knees, with my sleeping bag around me, praying before a bamboo bar with a half-torn map of the world on the wall behind. Even as I prayed, prostitutes in sheer white gowns were greeting customers and leading them into the depths of the place. But as I cried out to God, I felt the Lord's presence encircle me. Heaven was there, even in that place, and the glory of God fell on me, and then peace came over me, this unbelievable peace.

I kept praying like that for about fifteen or twenty minutes, and afterward I turned to Chris and said, "I'm going to make it now. I'm okay."

What I didn't know at the time was that on the other side of the divided world Deborah was praying for me right then in Washington, D.C. As we compared notes later, we found that she had been sitting on her couch in the basement of her parents' home, watching a televangelist. He said, "Lift your hands and ask in the name of Jesus for what's truly in your heart, believing with me that it will come to pass." So she prayed, "Lord Father, I cry out for Chauncey, for Chauncey's soul. I pray, Lord Father, that he gets born again in Africa."

The next day, two things happened. President Nixon resigned and our professor returned from his night of debauchery. He couldn't be bothered with apologizing and simply loaded us into a Land Rover and began the drive north to where the Kabre tribe lived.

Oppression: Spiritual and Physical

The Kabre people lived in round huts with thatch roofs on a high plane or the savannah. They were animists, believing that all things are inhabited by spirits, some good, many evil. Certain areas in the surrounding country were marked off by goats' and pigs' heads to signal the presence of evil spirits, warning against entry.

Despite my newfound faith, I took these beliefs as mere superstition, interesting only as artifacts of a primitive culture. I have now come to believe that I was entering a kingdom of darkness and was about to be slammed. I had at least some sense of this at the time, for I remember that odd things started happening to me, like falling into a pig sty and being covered with manure. I was freaked out that I would contract an infection.

I don't know if it was the pig sty or not, but I came down with amoebic dysentery. I begged my professor to be taken back to Lomé for treatment, but he kept saying my illness would pass. The other students and he were having too much fun partying and drinking. As for me, things were passing all right; in fact, *everything* I ate immediately exploded from my colon as if it were a fire hose, but the infection itself did not pass. I finally spotted a UN pickup that was returning to the city for a load of rice. I convinced the driver to give me a lift and strapped myself to the flatbed for the 250-mile ride.

This time, having secured my plane ticket and some money from my professor, I was able to rent a battered room in a hotel whose concrete walls made the place feel like a bunker. I asked at the desk for four cases of Coca-Cola to keep myself hydrated and went to the room to sweat the disease out. I asked for a doctor, only to have a voodoo practitioner appear. He shook his beads at me and wanted me to wear a necklace of chicken bones, but I waved him off, again and again, until he finally left.

After a period of delirium—which may have lasted as long as two weeks—I was joined by another sufferer. He and I kept each other some company, but we didn't improve much. I prayed for God's deliverance throughout this time, and I knew that my born-again experience was making a difference, even if I didn't fully appreciate that my disease might be the devil's way of coming against a new believer.

I was finally able to secure some antibiotics from another student on his travels and recovered.

I spent my last days in Togo ranging around the city, shopping in the local markets. One of the pieces that I bought was a round statuette with short arms that I thought Deborah might like.

When I finally landed back at Dulles Airport—after a scare about our landing gear—Deborah was there to meet me in her white MG. She knew immediately that I had changed. The tension that had been between us due to my lack of faith was now gone. We took off in the MG with the top down. We were young and in love and together.

Struggling Through School

Over the next two years, I attended Virginia Commonwealth University while Deborah went to Virginia Tech. I majored in anthropology and premed and did well, maintaining a B+ average. The greater part of the wave of baby boomers was coming of age at that time and applications to medical school were at an all-time high. Even in those last two years of school, I still hadn't gotten the message that I couldn't work every odd job that came to hand, pursue an active social life that included torturous trips over the mountain in my underpowered VW van to see Deborah, and still ace my studies and my Medical College Admission Tests. Again, I performed well on the MCATs but didn't achieve a score that would have trumped my B+ average. I did not get into medical school.

With my limited prospects, Deborah and I didn't marry upon graduation. We had not figured out how we could make a life together, and Deborah had a major health problem as well. Close to graduation, her appendix ruptured, spreading infection through-out her body. She almost died in the hospital. Her recovery was long and difficult and, as it would keep proving, incomplete. Obviously she didn't feel much like being a bride.

She began a job at the International Monetary Fund, where she retreated to the bathroom several times a day to inject herself with antibiotics.

I worked at odd jobs while I took selected advanced science classes at Georgetown University and George Washington University. I felt that if I could ace these tough classes, improve my GPA, and do better on the admission tests, I'd be accepted to medical school. But when I applied again, I was refused once more.

At that point Deborah and I had a talk. I asked her for one more year of preparation and a last shot at medical school. If I wasn't admitted again, I'd give up my plans of becoming a doctor.

By this time I understood that my checkered undergraduate record was a problem I'd have to find a way around. People some-times caught a break who worked close to the medical profession. A position as a lab assistant opened up at George Washington

University in the medical school's anatomy department. It meant doing all the scum work—the nasty, dirty work—involved in running the gross anatomy lab, in which first-year medical students dissect corpses.

I met with the professor in charge, Richard Snell, an Englishman. He told me he had already hired someone. I told him that my family had an English lineage, implying we were countrymen under the skin, and that I would work 300 percent harder than anyone else he could possibly have hired. That I would do exactly as asked, never complain, and prove brighter than any of his first-year med students. He knew I was desperate, and he could see from my record that I wouldn't be easily stopped; he hired me, dismissing the previous hire.

I spent that summer cleaning up the gross anatomy lab, which meant bagging all the corpses from the previous year that had been sliced, diced, probed, amputated, filleted, and finally left as piles of rotting mush in lymphatic goo. Then the stainless-steel examining gurneys had to be washed down, disinfected, and made spotless. I spent weeks going about these tasks between bouts of vomiting and dry heaving. I would eventually become more comfortable in this environment, but the smell never left me. Still, I never complained and eventually gained a reputation as the best lab assistant George Washington had ever seen.

When school began, I also took some graduate classes to further beef up my résumé.

I raised a concern only when I was asked to collect five-gallon buckets of fetuses from the women's hospital in D.C. I had to pour these out and label them. What I saw horrified me, as I thought some tragic mistake had been made and I had collected the remains of miscarriages, for many of the fetuses were nearly full-term—these were clearly babies. I went to Richard Snell and told him of the mistake. He followed me into the lab and explained, "No, this is perfectly normal. We get them all the time like this from the women's hospital." This was medicine? But I was too young and too intent on my ambitions to see that even great goods like modern medicine can be turned to evil ends. I felt it in my gut, though.

Caribbean Med

A professor at the school noticed my diligent work and suggested I might try a new medical school in the West Indies, St. George's University School of Medicine on the island of Grenada. The professor had been teaching down there—he was not sure the school was going to fly (they were then in only their second year of operation), but he thought it might be a good opportunity for me. Instruction was being given in English, so I wouldn't have to learn another language.

Several of the other graduate students and I were always comparing notes on how to get into medical school. One of them, Andrew, was keen on the Grenada idea and ready to go. He left to start his training there in the spring semester. If it worked out for him, I decided I would follow. His ensuing reports were entirely favorable.

With the prospect of medical school finally before us, Deborah and I married in the spring of 1978. She had still not fully recovered from her ruptured appendix, however, and had to undergo surgery a second time. We thought the surgery would take care of matters and she would make a complete recovery, but she remained ill during the early days of our marriage.

I had to leave for medical school in Grenada without her. We thought she'd recover in a matter of weeks and join me, but instead she was in and out of the hospital, fighting an infection that had, to date, fought off every antibiotic thrown at it.

I missed Deborah terribly, but I found myself right at home in medical school. Many of the other students found adjusting to conditions in Grenada difficult, but after sweating out amoebic dysentery in a hovel in Togo, I found Grenada a Caribbean paradise. I conceived a lifelong love for tropical landscapes, which is part of what makes me feel so much at home in Palm Beach now.

As my classes started, I found the material fascinating and realized—as I had hoped all along—that I was going to be a good doctor. I was as much in my element as the fish in the island's Sargasso Sea. Energized by the material, I could stay up until 2:00 a.m. studying, rise at 6:00 a.m., attend classes all day, study into the wee hours once more, and repeat the same procedure again and again. I was one of the top performers on midterms.

But Deborah's condition continued to be touch-and-go. As we talked on the phone I kept hoping I'd hear she had improved, but the news continued to be bad. Finally, I knew it would be wrong to stay away any longer. When we first started dating as kids, I had promised that I would never hurt her and always put her first, and I've always tried to keep that pledge. I knew I could start medical school again in the spring, and so I came back, found a part-time job, and helped nurse her back to health. My father was not pleased that my long-delayed medical plans were being set back further; that I had, in his view, wasted a semester. But I didn't want to be a doctor if it meant being apart from Deborah.

Deborah was able to come with me to Grenada for the spring semester, although she still wasn't entirely well. The doctors, having tried every full-spectrum antibiotic known, suggested that she complement her medications with traditional remedies like hot baths. It wasn't that easy to take a bath in Grenada. In order to take a soak Deborah had to heat water on the stove and pour it into a steel tub that we used for washing our clothes.

It was heavenly being together, but man, we were poor. Deborah found a job creating Sunday school materials for the missionaries, which made for a good atmosphere but paid very little. In my pride, I refused to write either of our parents for extra assistance when we could have used it, and during one memorable two-and-one-half-week stretch, I climbed palm trees every night to retrieve coconuts as a side dish to the little bags of rice we had for dinner.

Fortunately prayer—and our parents' intuitions of our financial situation—eventually prevailed and we began eating better.

I received world-class instruction at St. George's, because the opportunity to take a break and teach on a Caribbean island was attractive to many medical experts. But there was another big hurdle to jump. The first two years of medical school are devoted to classroom and lab work. The last one to two years involve doing rotations—six-week stints also known as clinical clerkships—through the various specialties, from internal medicine to dermatology to psychiatry, usually in the company of the heads of these units in a teaching hospital. That was the best juncture at which to make the leap back to the States, because then one could take the qualifying exams at home and be as much an American doctor as anybody else.

Yale

I had a friend named Mark Cullen who was from Connecticut. He had a son who was suffering from an immune disease and was in and out of the hospital at Saint Mary's in New Haven, where Yale's medical school students do their rotations. The faculty at Yale offered Mark the chance to do his rotations under their guidance so that he could be with his son.

That opened the door for me—or started to turn the knob. I went up to Yale one weekend during my last semester at St. George's and started banging on medical faculty doors. I was able to speak with an Englishman, Dr. Peter Fielding, who considered my request. As I had with Richard Snell, I appealed to Peter as a "fellow Englishman," at least by virtue of lineage. I told him that my wife was sick and I couldn't let her waste away in a third-world country anymore, so I had to come back to the States to do my clinical clerkships. If he'd just give me one rotation, I'd show him what I could do. I was Hippocrates, William Harvey, and Jonas Salk all rolled into one—at least in terms of St. George's graduates. He had to give me a chance!

He did. He allowed me to do a rotation with him in surgery. I imagine I didn't impress him as another Christiaan Barnard—the first doctor to do a heart transplant—but he thought well enough of my work to recommend me to his colleagues, and over the next two years I picked up all the rotations I needed. I went from being a medical student outside the United States to being a Yale-trained MD. While I was at it, I assisted Peter Fielding with his surgical research and began to see my future as a cardiologist.

Even after we reached Connecticut, Deborah continued

to struggle with her health. The doctors at Yale discovered that abscesses had formed—localized collections of infected pus surrounded by inflamed tissues—in her abdomen. Her appendectomy and her second surgery had created scar tissue that effectively walled off these areas of infection from the medication she had been taking—that's why she continued to struggle. Such a prolonged illness would have been a trial to anyone, but for Deborah it proved particularly difficult because of spiritual confusion.

Although she benefited greatly from most of the teaching of her charismatic mentors, they also introduced a false and destructive idea. They said that our faith could be strengthened and purified by trials, and so one ought to pray for a trial. Deborah had done so and thought, early on, that her ruptured appendix might have been God's way of answering this prayer. She did not understand that while God can use the trials Satan brings into our lives, God is never the author of these trials. God's will for us is to *enjoy* His loving presence. Deborah became so confused by God's failure to deliver her from a sickness she presumed He had brought about that she began to despair. What we should have done was unite with God in prayer—with as many others voicing intercessory prayers as possible—against the evil of her disease, in which no doubt Satan rejoiced.

Her doctors told her that they were going to have to perform yet another surgery. Her spiritual confusion was so great at that point that right before she went into surgery, she told God she wanted to die.

She heard God's voice ask, "Do you really want to die?"

She heard God's voice audibly, as she would hear anyone else's, and this shocked her. She suddenly realized what she was saying. The tone of God's voice implied that He was taking her seriously.

It wasn't a rhetorical question God was posing. Did she really want to die?

Her life had become so miserable with continued illness that she didn't have much love for life left, but she did know how I, her parents, and her brother would grieve. "No, God," she answered, "I suppose I don't really want to die."

The surgeons almost lost her on the operating table. When she woke up after the surgery, she told me that her left leg felt funny, like it was asleep. An orthopedist brought a stickpin. "Does that hurt? Does that?"

Her leg was paralyzed. One of the attending physicians had held a clamp too tight on a nerve during the operation.

She was determined not to be crippled, though, and began walking on that leg—or dragging it along—as soon as possible.

Deborah was not truly cured of her infection and its accompanying fevers until a woman from our church came to pray with her in our living room. Deborah told her that she had prayed and prayed and it hadn't done any good. The woman said that she had been healed of colitis and she wanted to pray with Deborah, believing that she would be healed. It was only after this prayer session that Deborah truly began to feel better and her infection dissipated.

Prayer Cellar

"Pray without ceasing" (1 Thess. 5:17 KJV)! We never know when in God's providence God will choose to heal us. We do know that Jesus tells us never to stop praying.

I learned a lot about prayer myself during those years at Yale.

Deborah and I lived in a little town outside New Haven called Woodbury. We belonged to a church that had a prayer room located in the root cellar of an old saltbox house, circa 1700. Many nights toward the end of my forty-five-minute drive home from the hospital, I'd stop by, open the slanted doors to the cellar, and spend time praying.

The cellar was so cramped that I couldn't stand up in it, and it was mostly unadorned, except for a desk, a lampstand, a Bible, a few devotional books, and a box of index cards with prayer requests written on them. I'd often be in there alone on dark nights, the New England winter howling around the house. I'd pick up a card, pray over the request, and go to the next.

Almost from the beginning of my Christian life, I attended Bible studies and prayer groups and benefited from them but still found myself slightly dissatisfied with all the talking about God. I wanted to meet God; to know God's love, God's power, God's presence. Talking about God with our fellow Christians is good, but prayer is the main conduit, the direct line, we have to God's power and glory. Go into your closet when you pray, Jesus tells us (Matt. 6:6). Praying in the root cellar I came to understand why.

I'd be in that damp-smelling, musty place, the dust of the beams as heavy as a prayer shawl, with the taste of the house's rusted pipes in my mouth—I'd be down there in the root cellar with now-empty mason jars and scatterings of nails and screws and a cracked and buckling floor, down there cold and still like a boxed cabbage, and God would show up. He would fling wide the night, hold aside the winds, steal through the slanted doors, and rest in my heart. Sometimes as I prayed, tears would come to my eyes for reasons I couldn't fathom.

Spiritual Interference

My MD certification in hand, I thought about doing my medical residence in surgery, in preparation for being a heart surgeon. Two things deterred me. Just as I was graduating one of the bright young surgical residents lost a patient because he hadn't learned enough about internal medicine. I never wanted that to happen to me. Also, Yale then had a pyramid system as a means of evaluating its surgical residents. Everyone was ranked, and no one was certified until he or she became the program's top resident. That meant you could remain a surgical resident, theoretically, forever. So I did my three-year residency at Yale in internal medicine.

In 1986, after my years at Yale, I went into cardiology at Mount Sinai Beth Israel Hospital in New York. As the name would suggest, Beth Israel is mostly a Jewish hospital, and I was one of the few Gentile doctors there. I have a great love for the Jews and tremendous respect for their culture, as any Christian should since we are "grafted into" the vine of Israel (Rom. 11:17–24).

When we moved to New York, Deborah studied at Parsons design school for a year and then went to work for a graphic design firm. She was fulfilling her artistic ambitions at last. She was still struggling, though, in her recovery from the paralysis in her leg brought on by her last surgery. She was exiting a bus one day, forgot about her leg not working well, and fell hard down the bus's steps onto the sidewalk. Being Deborah, she promptly picked herself up and commanded her leg to behave.

Her greatest frustration was in not being able to have children. Even though she wasn't well when we first married, we wanted children right away. She had been trying to become pregnant for eight years. We did not know if she ever would become pregnant because of the damage caused by her ruptured appendix. That could well have made her infertile.

Then she conceived and had a miscarriage.

She conceived once more, and this pregnancy advanced into the third month, but an ultrasound revealed the pregnancy to be ectopic. The baby was growing outside the womb, attached to a major artery. The surgery meant to save her life almost ended it, as the artery exploded the moment the surgeons began the procedure. Her bleeding resembled that of a gunshot wound, they told her.

God implants a desire for children deep within a woman's heart. And both of us wanted life to come from the love we shared. At times Deborah thought about almost nothing else, night and day. Our marriage began to suffer as Deborah was inconsolable and I found myself frustrated at watching her suffer and not being able to do anything about it.

What good was being a doctor if I couldn't help the one I loved above all others? Why wouldn't God bless us with children? Deborah had even had an experience in which she felt quite distinctly that God was going to give us children, but as the years went on this became harder and harder to believe.

One day Deborah's brother called. He had become a minister and had just finished attending a seminar out west. "You know that little statue you have on your bedside table?"

"Yes."

"I think you should get rid of it. That's a fertility goddess. A voodoo fetish. This seminar was about spiritual warfare. The speaker said that sometimes the most innocuous-looking things—like your statue—can be used by the devil to gain entry into a home and cause spiritual oppression."

Deborah's brother tends to be more a rationalist than either Deborah or I am, and Deborah couldn't believe what she was hearing. "It's an art object. It's not a...whatever you called it. Chauncey picked it up in Togo. I've been hanging my jewelry on it for years."

"Exactly. That's why you should get rid of it."

When I came home, Deborah told me what her brother had said and suggested we get rid of the statuette.

"But I gave that to you. It's one of my nice memories from that trip."

"My brother said it could be the reason I'm not getting pregnant."

I thought of all the medical reasons this was complete hogwash. But my wife was upset and I thought it best to oblige her. "Okay. Let's do it. And let's do it right." What did I care about a reminder of Togo, voodoo capital of the world?

We lived on the twenty-first floor of an apartment building. There was a trash chute that led from our apartment down to the basement and an incinerator. I took the little statue and smashed it up in pieces, threw every bit of it down the chute, and prayed, "In the name of Jesus Christ, if any spiritual oppression has come to this house as a result of this statue, let it be gone." Or words to that effect.

Within two weeks Deborah was pregnant with twins.

Game, Set, Match

As our twins fought for the club's junior tennis championship, Deborah and I realized, as an outside observer could never know, how much our boys had been longed for and prayed for—how much we cherished them. We cherished them so dearly in their early years, in fact, that we came close to making idols out of them. Christian, the dark-haired one, boisterous, protector of his shy brother, hands gifted for working with mechanical things—a born engineer or doctor; Chad, with his sandy hair, the artistic one, who wanted to play out every story he fell in love with and so took up the violin after learning of one of the instrument's masters, becoming accomplished in no time. Such a pair!

They did not spare each other on the court, though, as the match went to a third set and then a tiebreaker. After Chad's illness, it was hard not to root a little harder for him. What if the illness returned? How many chances in life would he have? But it was also hard not to root for Christian, as he was clearly the underdog. Chad would keep playing whatever happened; he was obsessed. Maybe a victory would give Christian the impetus he needed to be serious about the sport in the way Chad was.

They battled, in McEnroe-Borg fashion, to a 16–14 finish. For the longest time neither could manage the win and neither would accept the loss. A super, running, down-the-line forehand finally gave Chad the victory.

We jumped on the court and took them both into our arms.

I told Christian I was never prouder of him.

Deborah whispered into Chad's ear, "You just won Wimbledon."

CHAPTER 7

Why Chad?

One day after Deborah had brought Chad home from the tennis courts, he was clearing out his tennis racquets, clothing bag, and other paraphernalia from the family Range Rover, which included a portable but heavy ball machine. The machine pitched out balls from one side of the court to the other and could be adjusted for height, spin, and direction, which allowed Chad to hit one hundred forehands in a row or alternating shots from either wing, and approach shots and volleys as well. When he lifted the machine out of the car, Chad crumpled to the driveway in pain, screaming. A rib on his right side had snapped.

I was at home and settled him down. A cracked rib is often more uncomfortable than painful, as the fracture constricts breathing and every intake of air brings a feeling of pressure and shortness of breath. But Chad's face was drawn with a pain that wasn't letting up. We took him to the hospital for X-rays.

The underlying pain, it turned out, came from a tumor. His

leukemia had metastasized, producing the tumor, which likely meant that another line of stem cells had turned cancerous—a line that was escaping Gleevec's control. I knew Chad was really in trouble now. As I've noted, once CML spreads to a second line of stem cells capable of producing tumors, a development that's as rare as it is potentially lethal, a patient's life expectancy greatly diminishes. I could analyze this objectively as a doctor, but as a father I was simply devastated. Chad had enjoyed two and a half relatively good years since his diagnosis. So much so that at one point I had become convinced that he was healed and had taken him off the Gleevec. His blood work kept coming back for so many weeks in a row with no trace of cancer that I convinced myself, if only for a time, that God had worked a definitive miracle and Chad was healed. But before he started to grow pale and his muscles slacken again, I thought better of this and put him back on the medication. He had been taking the medication and doing fine before the tumor appeared—or so we thought.

Why was this happening to him? Chad couldn't help but wonder. He asked, *Why me?* as anyone would. What had he done to deserve CML?

Of course, he hadn't done anything even remotely deserving of cancer. I searched for causes in the natural order, noting that leukemia had struck three other children in our neighborhood, potentially constituting what the Centers for Disease Control would call a "cluster." We live close to the nearby airport and the jets put a lot of benzene in the air, a cancer-causing agent. Then, too, Palm Beach was undergoing a huge public works project, with old sewer and water lines being taken out and replaced by new ones. For decades the manicured yards and gardens of the Palm Beach mansions had been lavished with carcinogenic pesticides, in the days before there were any environmental controls. All the digging no doubt released a swarm of toxins into the air.

Still, it was Chad that was sick. Not me, not Deborah, not Christian. Why Chad? Was it only chance? If so, what meaning did any of our lives have, if Chad's life didn't have a meaning that went beyond the luck of the draw? Either there's a purpose for each of us that's greater than what we can invent for ourselves or the existence of God is a hoax.

When Chad asked, *Why me?* he presumed, as most of us do, that his suffering had come upon him as a punishment. We think God has done this to us. God has cursed us. God harbors a vindictive streak against us for reasons we can only suspect but never know.

Chad was chosen, I have come to believe, as Job was chosen. Not for any misdeed he had committed but for his virtue and spiritual giftedness. He was not chosen by God to be a victim of leukemia. God doesn't afflict anyone with such wickedness. He was chosen by Satan, because Satan wanted to destroy a child God had blessed—a child who might win victories for God's kingdom. In the bargain, he wanted to destroy the faith of the child's parents and his brother and anyone who had ever been affected by Chad's life, tempting us to blame God for the manifest and hideous injustice of Chad's illness. Curse God and die, Job's wife advised (Job 2:9). That's Satan's wicked message—a spiritual contagion borne along with every distortion of God's creation, all the illness and injustice and poverty and poisonous thinking and every other form of wickedness through which Satan, the prince of this world, binds and blights creation.

Satan came against Job because he was exemplary. The devil claimed that Job worshiped God only because God had blessed him. Job would curse God the minute those blessings were removed.

Satan expected that Chad would curse God, the Crandalls would curse God, the minute this precious young man was afflicted. Or somewhere along the way in the grinding, painful, exhausting, grueling, torturing, and terrorizing business of receiving treatment for cancer. That was the devil's plan.

I couldn't have said any of this then. Nor could Chad. It's part of Satan's strategy to produce utter confusion and bewilderment and even the thought and feeling that one has been deserted by God.

Chad's Struggles and Spiritual Strengths

But let me tell you about Chad. Our twins were raised on Bible stories. Deborah was constantly reading to them from a children's Bible, and their favorite videos were animated versions of Noah's ark, Joseph and his coat of many colors, and God calling to Samuel. They loved hearing the prophet Eli instructing Samuel that the next time the Lord spoke, he should reply, "Speak, LORD, for your servant is listening" (1 Sam. 3:9 NIV).

Deborah was also heavily involved in Bible Study Fellowship, which takes people through a detailed exposition of the Scriptures so that they know the Bible's substance thoroughly. When we were in Richmond, as the boys grew from infants to toddlers to preschoolers, they would go to Deborah's Bible Study Fellowship meetings, where child care was provided, with the same lessons taught to the children that were being taught to the adults. When Christian and Chad started attending a secular preschool, they didn't like it nearly as much as Bible Study Fellowship. In fact, when their preschool teacher decorated the classroom for Halloween with silhouettes of witches on broomsticks, leering jack-o'-lanterns, and spiders and their webs, Christian and Chad were horrified. Christian pulled at Deborah's pants leg and said, "Tell the teacher. You have to give the day to God. Tell her, Mommy. You have to give the day to God!"

The teacher answered Deborah's questions about glorifying the darkness by saying, "Well, they know it's not real, don't they?"

Images of evil spiritual forces may be innocently used as Halloween decorations, but that doesn't mean such powers aren't real. They are very real indeed, as our boys knew.

Chad had a particularly lively imagination and he was drawn to imitate admirable characters. He wanted to live out the stories he came to love. So, when the story of David and Goliath captured his imagination, nothing would do but that he receive a slingshot for Christmas. He marched around the house shooting tiny wads of paper at imaginary Goliaths for weeks.

Later, as I've mentioned, when he fell in love with the story of the great violinist Paganini, he devoted himself to the violin and quickly became the pride of his Suzuki class. By the time he reached adolescence, he played so well that I enjoyed listening to him practice.

He inherited Deborah's artistic talents in double measure and drew well even as a very small child. He drew lots of common cartoon images but with a twist that expressed his sense of humor, like putting glasses on Superman. Christian did not have the same ability and became jealous of the praise Chad won for his pictures once they reached grammar school. Chad helped solve this crisis by teaching Christian to draw a pirate, and Christian's drawing ended up winning first prize in a school contest.

There was an unaccountable and even mysterious side to Chad that I did not understand well as he grew up. He tended to be fearful in ways that appeared to be early signs of neurosis. He shunned any direct light, for instance, and would even skew his ball cap to one side to guard against the sun shining on his face. We took him to a psychiatrist about this, who found herself at a loss. Eventually, I asked a wise Christian woman what she thought. She asked me, in turn, whether he had been in an incubator as an infant. He had, since he was jaundiced when first born—a bilirubin baby, as they're called. She told me she saw this all the time. She explained the situation to Chad: he had been frightened of the lights he had been put under when he was first born. Now he needn't be frightened anymore. Then she prayed over him. After that, this peculiar fear vanished.

Chad had other fears, though, fears that were not so easily cured and probably should not have been, because they were grounded in perceptions that were more real than we knew. He had terrible nightmares and he claimed to see evil presences—wolves and demons. We thought he was only afraid of the dark and the unknown like any other child. But now that I've met other people who have a heightened sense of the spiritual world all around us, I'm not so sure. Just as I'm convinced that demons are real now, I'm convinced that there are people who get a glimpse of them now and again. I don't mean to be spooky or kooky. But there are more things in heaven and earth than are realized in the way most of us look at life.

I remember all too well that one morning before Chad's diagnosis he awoke from a nightmare and came screaming into the family room, where he announced that he had leukemia. As good parents, Deborah and I told Chad that he shouldn't even say that.

He had just had a nightmare. We thought the news of another child close by dying of leukemia had caught up to Chad. We were so grateful that our son did not have leukemia. But, in fact, he did. Who knows where that dream came from?

What we thought were Chad's childish fears contrasted with his otherwise mature behavior. He was not only well-behaved but a boy who was liked by both his peers and adults, even during the difficult early teen years. Chad was such a favorite at the tennis club that adults often asked him to hit with them or fill out a threesome for a doubles match.

Sensitive, artistic, well-behaved, a charmer with a heart for God: why wouldn't Satan want to destroy him? Not just his life but everything he meant to those who knew him—the sign Chad was of God's goodness.

A Children's Story—or Something Else?

The devil went after Chad even earlier than we knew. What I've been slowly learning is that the father of lies can use many seemingly innocuous things—like the fertility statue I brought back from Togo. In Chad's case, evil used a charming story, a staple of children's literature, *Peter Pan*. Chad fell in love with the story and insisted on a Peter Pan outfit for Christmas, complete with the long green shirt, green tights, a pointed, green feathered cap, and the pipes that Peter played.

Peter Pan evokes in most only a desire to remain young or the wish to believe in wonderfully imaginative creatures like fairies. But the story's underlying basis has dark elements. J. M. Barrie, the author of the original play, *Peter Pan*, based the character in part on a little boy he knew and in part on the Greek god Pan.[1] Pan is a god of music and of the forest. That sounds charming, but he's also a god of fear (the basis of our word *panic*). He is depicted as half man, half goat, with horns, hairy legs, and cloven feet. He is the archetype for many Christian images of Satan.[2]

J. M. Barrie's relationship with the children on whom he based the characters in his play—the five sons of Arthur Llewellyn Davies—would raise alarms today, as he took a stomach-turning pleasure, to judge by his novel *The Little White Bird*, in giving a child a bath. Two of the five boys eventually committed suicide: the fourth boy, Michael, drowned in what was believed to be a suicide pact with his best friend. The model for Peter Pan himself, the second son, Peter Llewellyn Davies, threw himself under a train at the age of sixty-three, having been haunted by the specter of Peter Pan his entire life.[3]

Deborah and I were completely unaware of all this until I began discussing Chad's fears with an evangelist from Colombia, Randy McMillan. He asked me about Chad's childhood, in detail, going through every stage of his development. When I told him about Chad's fascination with Peter Pan, he said, "That's it! You have to get everything out of this house that has anything to do with Peter Pan!"

At first I reacted as I had with the Togo statue. Chad had had no interest in his old Peter Pan stuff for years. I thought Randy was making way too much out of a children's story.

But that night I went online and found out everything I could about the basis of Peter Pan. I stayed up until 3:00 a.m. I started weeping as I sat in front of the computer. I said, "Lord, I can't believe this. I let this in the house. Forgive me."

I woke up the next morning and talked to Deborah. We

ransacked the house to find everything that had to do with Peter Pan. I got all the Peter Pan books. I found the costume's leotards. I found the hat, the flute. I took this paraphernalia into the backyard, put it in a metal bucket, poured gasoline on it, and burned it. I cried out as it burned, "You devil, you're not allowed in my house. You're not allowed to attack my son. If this fear came into my house through this garbage, it has to go today, in Jesus' name."

I walked into the house and Chad said, "Dad, all my fears are gone. All my fear is gone!"

Once again, as with the statue from Togo, the Lord was telling us, "This stuff is real. Most people won't believe it, but you *must!*"

How I wish I had understood at that point—and even earlier in Chad's life—the spiritual battle in which life consists. This is not being kooky, albeit some can go overboard in attributing everything to the devil and demons. If I had realized the spiritual authority a Christian father has over his family, if I had understood then, as I do now, how powerful fasting and prayer can be in combating wickedness, including the evil of disease, I would have been much bolder in praying with Chad and commanding the fears oppressing him to leave, in Jesus' name.

Also, I would not have taken such a clinical approach to the situation, trying to see his fears in terms of childhood development and related psychiatric issues. I would have taken him in my arms! When he was afraid, I would have held him and assured him that God was standing with us against his oppressive fears. I would have accepted what was happening as real and tried to understand the spiritual vision he had been given. That would have helped him, I think, much more than telling him he was foolish and possibly crazy. I would just have loved on him!

A Dream of Hell

During Chad's illness, I had a dream that was so vivid it might be called a vision—one that taught me to have greater respect for the supernatural. In the dream I was walking into a barn. The barn had three levels to it, and I pulled myself easily up into the second-story loft. When I tried to get into the level above that, I found myself struggling, and when I arrived I sensed an overwhelming evil presence. I grabbed a nearby bucket. When I did a door blew open with a raging fire behind it, and the fire reached out toward me and seemed to grab the bucket, threatening to pull me along with it into the fire. If I wasn't in hell at that moment, I'm certain that I was being given a vision of hell, and a sense of hell's desire to destroy me. I held on to the bucket for a while, resisting the pull of the fire with all my might, but finally I let the bucket go into the fire and was able to walk out of the barn.

At that point, I woke up screaming. Where was Deborah? I started praying immediately, and I wanted her to pray with me. I have never been so terrified. "Deborah!" I called out. "Deborah! Pray!"

The door to the bathroom opened. Deborah came out. "I have been praying," she said. It turned out that while I was having a dream-vision of hell, Deborah had been on her knees in the darkened bathroom, interceding for Chad. She had been praying when the devil unleashed the power of fear against me. I think the message he wanted me to receive was this: "This is all too much for you; you are in danger of losing your mind. Put all of this religious fanaticism aside. Forget about it, or you may find yourself destroyed by what you are imagining or what's more real than you want to know."

That dream was a sign of evil's reality, and now I believe Chad's "childish nightmares" were, too.

Problems in Houston

With the appearance of the tumor, Chad's doctors in Florida doubled his dose of Gleevec. This had some effect at first, but then Chad's white blood cell counts started climbing at an alarming rate. Gleevec—our silver bullet—wasn't working anymore. I had continued to research the treatment of leukemia in children and found a physician at M. D. Anderson Children's Cancer Hospital in Houston who was particularly knowledgeable and sounded welcoming on the phone, should Chad need hospitalization. With Chad's counts climbing and Gleevec ineffective, Chad's only hope was in new courses of therapy. In the fall of 2003, at the beginning of the school year, we flew as a family to Houston, where Chad began a massive course of chemotherapy.

We hoped to stay in Houston together as a family. I rented an apartment in the Museum Tower, a complex close to the hospital. It was bright and cheerful, and I spent a lot of money furnishing it. I wanted to provide a semblance of home to Chad, as he would be in and out of the hospital during his chemotherapy treatments, and to Christian, as he would be homeschooled by Deborah. That was our initial plan.

It quickly became apparent, however, that hanging around M. D. Anderson, with its hundreds of severely afflicted children, was no place for Christian. What's more, Chad's care consumed all Deborah's time. We were kidding ourselves if we thought she was going to be able to homeschool Christian.

We decided to enroll Christian in a boarding school, Saint Andrew's, in Boca Raton, Florida. Christian had had enough of seeing his brother suffer and his parents obsessed with his care.

Christian's new digs at Saint Andrew's were as commodious as boarding schools come, but Deborah and I couldn't help feel—as I'm sure Christian did as well—that we were abandoning him. Christian was called upon to make many sacrifices for his brother, especially in terms of his parents' attention. There was little we could do about this, and at the same time we knew that Christian, as a fourteen-year-old, couldn't help feeling cheated.

The devastating illness of a child has a major impact on a family and each member in it. It distorts the way each person relates to other family members, and that's why many families don't survive the death of a child intact—everyone suffers, grieves, and feels resentful, because there's no real balancing of accounts, no justice in the meting out of love. Christian came through this period remarkably well, but as I remember dropping him off at school, saying good-bye, talking with him later as he adapted to his new surroundings, I think of how tough what the family went through was on him. So I pause for a moment in a personal aside to say that your mother and I loved you as best we could during those days, Christian. And you were soon to respond bravely to the even greater demands we would place upon you.

Christian's Sacrifice

Chad's massive round of chemotherapy at M. D. Anderson had the desired effect of reducing his white count, but only during the actual course of treatment. His leukemia attacked again as the terrorizing cells came out of hiding. The doctors found leukemia in his spinal fluid, and this was such a bad sign that they wondered if anything more could be done other than palliative care—simply treating Chad's pain.

By this time Deborah and I were ready to consider a bone marrow transplant. Chad's doctors wondered if he could survive the procedure. I argued that he was strong—I knew that his body still had an underlying strength because of his fitness as a tennis player. I pressed the staff at M. D. Anderson to let Chad receive a bone marrow transplant from his brother, Christian, and they finally agreed. I'm pretty sure they thought Chad wouldn't survive the procedure.

We had resisted a bone marrow transplant for so long because of the risks, as I've said. The procedure has nasty effects on the donor as well, and I knew too well what Christian was facing when I picked him up from Saint Andrew's and brought him once more to Houston.

Christian received injections for a week prior to the transplant that encouraged the production of stem cells. A fourteen-year-old boy has a healthy quantity of stem cells to begin with. The shots resulted in the hyperproduction of stem cells, causing joint pain. This can't be avoided, but it's no fun to go through. Christian was in a lot of pain. As Christ gave His blood for the life of the world, Christian was being asked to give his blood, his marrow, the life within him for his brother.

As Christian was being turned into a stem cell factory, Chad received more chemotherapy and then his body was irradiated, destroying his stem cells and his entire immune system. In a controlled manner, the doctors had performed the equivalent of exposing Chad to a Hiroshima, a nuclear blast. He was then isolated in a clean room, as his body would be unable to fight off the least infection. He was, in fact, slowly dying from the therapy itself, as the elimination of his diseased stem cells entailed destroying his normal stem cells as well. Unless the transplant worked, he'd be unable to produce any blood cells at all.

Once the injections had done their work in Christian's body, he was hooked up to a filtration system that harvested his stem cells as his blood was recycled. The nurse put a huge IV in one arm and a huge IV in the other arm and sent his blood from one vein through the machine into another vein. Or that was what was supposed to happen.

After the beginning of the procedure, I went to check on Deborah, who was watching over Chad in the clean room. When I returned to see about Christian, he was screaming. He was tied down to the table in a cruciform posture, each arm out to the side, and he could barely lift his head. But once he heard my voice in the room, he directed his cries at me. "Dad! They are killing me! They are killing me! Help me!"

The nurse was cooing, "Oh, he's all right. He's all right."

But I saw that the return IV hadn't been properly inserted, and his blood was not flowing back into his vein but diffusing through the flesh of his arm, which had by then swollen to the size of a ham. "You're infiltrating him!" I screamed to the nurse. "Can't you see that?"

She quickly removed the IVs and suspended the procedure. Christian lay strapped to the gurney, writhing in pain and fighting his tears.

I called up the supervising physician and let him have it. "You're M. D. Anderson. You're supposed to be the best in the world! How in the world can we trust you? I want an incident report filled out about this."

Accidents in medicine happen—all the time. I'm more apprecia-
tive now of what my patients tell me about their difficult experiences and attentive to their reactions. I warn myself against being
dismissive because things can go awry in a hurry and, particularly
in cardiology, there's no room for error. Right then I experienced
in full measure what any distraught parent would, my love of the
medical profession notwithstanding.

The hardest thing was telling Christian he would have to go
through the same procedure again. "Dad, they were trying to kill
me in there," he said. "I can't go through that again!"

I had to explain that not only would he have to go through it
again, he'd have to be reprepped with more injections to boost his
stem cell production. The joint pain would come back over the
weekend. But at the beginning of the next week, when they harvested his stem cells again, I'd be there. Every moment.

And I was, and this time I saw to it that the IVs were inserted
properly. Christian didn't experience anything worse than discom-
fort and impatience as his blood was cycled and his stem cells harvested over a period of three to four hours.

But he was off balance for the next week, as the procedure
destroyed his emotional equilibrium. He was disoriented and
imagined things: anxious at one moment, enraged the next, finding himself weeping and lost. He could not be reasoned with. We
just had to hold on to him until the normal balance of his blood
chemistry was restored. Christian had done such a brave thing,
but he was hardly aware of it for days afterward. After all he'd been
through, taking him back to the boarding school was one of the
hardest things I'd ever done.

Chad's long nightmare went on even as Christian's stem cells
were finding their way into Chad's bone marrow and regenerating

his blood supply and his immune system. Chad was nauseated and couldn't eat for a couple of weeks, as the radiation continued to destroy cells and his body struggled to cope with this living death. White sores formed on his lips and around his mouth. The only nourishment he was able to take was through an IV.

During this time, Deborah and I became even more radical in our prayers. We prayed over the blood transfusions that carried Christian's stem cells into Chad. "Lord, Father, give new life to our boy. In the name of Jesus we command all abnormal cells to die, and Lord, Father, we ask that these stem cells bring life to Chad. In Your Scriptures, You tell us that life is found in the marrow. May this bone marrow bring life to our son, Holy God. Honor our prayer, Lord, Father. In the name of Jesus."

Every time a new bag of "ringers" came in—fluids enriched with electrolytes administered by IV—and every time a new medication came in, I'd grab it from the nurse and pray over it. "Father God, in the name of Jesus, I pray over this, that no harm will come to my son, that only life will come into his body." Then I'd place sticky notes on the bag, with Bible verses like this one from the book of Acts: "God anointed Jesus of Nazareth with the Holy Ghost and with power: who went about doing good, and healing all" (10:38 KJV).

Writing on the Wall

After the transplant, Chad stayed in his hospital room for a month. He gradually improved, making steady progress. He began to eat on his own again, although he could keep down only the blandest food imaginable.

Deborah stayed with him night and day. She was the mother lion, fighting for her cub. I burned out occasionally and had to retreat to the apartment for rest. Once I went to the apartment in the afternoon, took a nap, then showered and returned in the early evening. I spruced up, put on a jacket and tie, and slapped on some cologne, thinking I'd take Deborah out to dinner—or at least to the commissary.

When I entered Chad's room, I came to the side of his bed and greeted him, "Hey, buddy."

He immediately started vomiting. Once he had thrown up the little in his stomach, he continued to retch, dry heaving. He waved me away between gags. "Your cologne! I can't take it. Get out of the room!"

Deborah, as mother lion, simply roared: "Do you know how hard we've worked to get his stomach settled? Look at him! How long do you think it's going to be before he can eat again? How will he get better? You had to know what that cologne would do to him. What were you thinking?"

I muttered about trying to freshen up and make it nice for everyone as I skipped back out the door.

That's what a month of watching a fourteen-year-old hang between life and death will do to you—and what the frustrations that build up can do to a couple. Deborah and I were both emotionally exhausted. We wondered why God was taking so long answering our prayers. We wondered whether God was with us at all. Could there be any meaning to Chad's suffering? What could possibly be accomplished through it that could justify so much hurt and pain?

M. D. Anderson takes in many patients from overseas, particularly from Saudi Arabia. The parents of these Muslim children would spread out their prayer rugs in their rooms and pray all day, crying out to Allah for the lives of their children. Deborah and I had no one at that time who would pray for us—we felt alone. I'd send out e-mail blasts and sometimes receive encouraging notes, which were tremendously appreciated, but the bedside of a sick child must be one of the loneliest places on earth, even when you are standing right next to the wife you love more than life itself. Grief and fear seemed our only company; so much so that we began losing the will to reach out to each other, if not to God. In those moments following the cologne fracas, I was wasted; I was at the bottom.

I went to the bathroom and washed off the scent. When I came back into Chad's room, the nurse asked me, "Dr. Crandall, where's the prayer on the wall?"

I didn't know what she meant.

"Right there, opposite the foot of his bed. Every day when I come in there's a prayer written on that wall. Something from the Word of God—Bible verses, but like a prayer. The other nurses and I talk about it at lunch. We don't know quite how you do it. The cleaning people talk about it. But you haven't written anything there today."

"I've never written anything on the wall," I said.

"Oh yes, you have. Stop kidding me."

"No, I haven't."

"Well, I'm not making it up. You wait a minute." The nurse went out and brought in another nurse. "Tell him," she said.

The other nurse commented that she had seen the prayers, too. A new one. Every day.

Deborah turned to me from where she was sitting beside Chad's bed, tears welling in her eyes. "God must've been here. He was here and we didn't even know it. We couldn't see it. But everyone who came in here could. They could read the Word of God on the wall."

I looked at Deborah and I worried that if I started then, I'd cry so hard I'd *howl*. I wanted to hold her, but I was afraid to.

"Strife broke the anointing," she said, her eyes downcast. "But God's been here—all the time."

CHAPTER 8

The Battle

After the bone marrow transplant, Chad made steady improvement. He gained weight and his color started coming back. When his blood counts improved sufficiently, we flew back home, with a sense of tremendous gratitude. The bone marrow transplant turned out not to be that bad after all, we thought. Slowly, we gained confidence that Chad was going to make it—that this nightmare was coming to an end. Once home, Chad was able to take part in a wedding and soon thereafter was back hitting tennis balls.

What Chad and the rest of the family had been through at M. D. Anderson taught us so much about practicing our faith in the midst of a battle with evil. Cancer is an evil; just because you can see malignant cells under a microscope doesn't mean they aren't an expression of Satan's will to destroy God's creation. The thorns on a vine, which anyone can see with the naked eye, are the result of evil influence, as Genesis tells us (3:18). Satan comes to kill, steal, and destroy. Cancer is a demonic spirit; like so many things that reflect Satan's character, cancer takes a good thing—cell reproduction—and introduces subtle twists that make it destructive, in fact, a killing machine.

Cancer opens one's eyes, in a sense, to the spiritual battle in which we are all engaged at every moment. When are we *not* being assaulted, in one way or another, by evil? It's vital that we learn to act on what God tells us—to play our part in the establishment of God's kingdom—even as we suffer all "the wiles of the devil" (Eph. 6:11 KJV).

As much of our time at M. D. Anderson was spent waiting— waiting between tests, for the next treatment, for enough time to pass for another procedure to be performed—I became restless and felt called to be doing the Lord's work in some way if I couldn't be helping patients as a doctor.

One of the books I was reading about miraculous healing, *How to Heal the Sick,* was written by Charles and Frances Hunter. I found their ministry was based just outside Houston in a northern suburb called Kingwood. Charles and Frances have often been called the "healing Hunters" and were used greatly in the charismatic movement of the 1970s and since.

Being a pushy kind of guy, I called Frances Hunter one day out of the blue. "Frances," I said, "I don't know you, but I need your help. My son is sick, and all I want to do is volunteer for your ministry. Can we do that? If it's okay, I'll bring him to you, let him rest in a sleeping bag, and we will do whatever you want us to do."

Frances said, "Sure, come ahead. We'll pray for him."

We Don't Have to Fight Alone

The first time we visited the Hunters, Christian as well as Chad was with us, and the four of us went together. The Hunters took one look at Chad and said, "You can have our bed." They had a small office with a daybed where they would sometimes take naps in the afternoons. We felt that daybed had a special anointing on it—it was a prophet's bed. Chad camped out there while the rest of us worked.

We helped the Hunters send out books, tapes, and CDs from their ministry. My son Christian loved burning the disks, and he spent hours manufacturing copies of the Hunters' video and audio presentations.

Others worked in the offices as well, of course, and the core group of people associated with the ministry came to know Chad and love him. They'd often prepare special dishes for him. And the Hunters, the other workers, and we would pray over Chad every day.

At one point, Chad had a frozen shoulder from the radiation. "Frozen shoulder" might not sound like a serious diagnosis, but anyone who has ever had one knows what a world of problems it can cause and how painful such a condition can be. Otherwise healthy adults with frozen shoulders find it agonizing. Chad could not raise his right arm at all, and this was particularly dispiriting to him as it meant he could not play tennis, even if his CML went into remission.

One day Charles Hunter walked right up to where Chad was lying, and he asked, "Chad, do you want that shoulder healed so that you can use it?"

Chad said, "Yes, sir."

"I'm going to pray for your shoulder, that it will be healed today."
He put both his hands on Chad's shoulder and cried out in the
name of Jesus for Chad to be healed. I'm not sure what inspired
him to do this; he must have been particularly convinced through
his prayers that God had appointed this day for the healing of
Chad's shoulder.

With Charles Hunter's prayer, by the power of God, Chad's frozen shoulder came loose, and he could use it normally once more.
Chad's eyes nearly popped out of his head and his faith lifted up.

Every extra moment we had while we were in Houston, we took
the family to the Hunters' ministry and worked. We were in a battle, and if we were in a battle we were going to fight it, and part of
fighting it meant doing the work of the Lord on behalf of others.
Soldiers fight not merely to survive but to prevail in the service of
those they are protecting over the enemy. We had to adopt this
attitude ourselves.

Through our work with the Hunters we learned—to our great
relief—that we did not have to fight the battle alone and should
not try. I remember the lonely days at M. D. Anderson as I watched
Muslims pray together constantly for their children—how abandoned I felt; how alone I felt with no one to pray with me other
than Deborah. But as we reached out to the Hunters, other Christians began reaching out to us.

Fellow Soldiers

Initially, the ministry of others came to us through books, as with
the Hunters. Deborah was particularly helped by Dodie Osteen's

book, *Healed of Cancer*—the story of her own battle with the disease. *Healed of Cancer* is filled with Bible verses about God's healing work, and Deborah ended up memorizing almost all these verses through constantly repeating them in her prayers. Dodie Osteen is the mother of Joel Osteen, the pastor of the huge Lakewood Church in Houston, and because of her book we contacted the church and an associate pastor named Steve came to pray with us, which was tremendously helpful.

I was especially helped, as I've mentioned, by T. L. Osborn's book *Healing the Sick* and Reinhard Bonnke's *Mighty Manifestations*. At the time I first started reading these books I had no idea I would soon become friends with people like the Hunters and Pastor Bonnke.

Once we met the Hunters, though, and understood what a difference Christian community could make in our struggle, we became so eager to know and pray with other Christians that we bought a second little house close by our own where missionaries could stay on short furloughs and other men and women of God could visit us.

Looking back, I see that I had been running after everything God could give me since the onset of Chad's illness. I wanted to be reassured of God's power by meeting missionaries and others who had experienced it. I encountered David Hogan and was literally "blown back" by the power of the Holy Spirit. I journeyed to Mexico to join Greg Rider and his team as they took the gospel to tribal peoples. But in these first inquiries, I was most concerned to see God work directly in ways that would convince me that God had the power and will to heal today, just as we read in the Bible.

Later, as the battle unfolded, I became more concerned to *join with* others in fighting the battle. I started seeing Chad's illness as part of the greater battle to make manifest God's goodness on the earth—the battle all Christians are called to fight together. Once Deborah and I became eager to join with our fellow Christians in God's work, God sent a virtual army of people to pray with us, often in surprising ways.

Prayer Army

Joel Stockstill, the pastor of Bethany World Prayer Center, a church that has three campuses in Baton Rouge, Louisiana, came to our area to preach at the small Jupiter, Florida, church. Joel was a young man in his mid- to late twenties. The circumstances of his appearance at the Jupiter church were peculiar, because he preaches regularly to thousands and he found himself this day appearing before a congregation so small it could not pay his trip expenses. The Lord told him to accept the invitation, so he did.

After his powerful sermon, the minister had to take off, and Joel was left standing alone but for his four huge, African-American bodyguards: Big Mike, Floyd, and two others. (That he felt it necessary to travel with an entourage of four suggested the need for crowd control at his usual venues.)

I felt as if God was telling me to honor this man of God, and I asked Joel and his bodyguards to the best place in town for lunch, the Breakers Hotel. Pastor Joel Stockstill impressed me as someone with wisdom way beyond his years. His wisdom came from study of the Scriptures—a study that he conducted even as he suffered from a debilitating illness. He had been on kidney dialysis since the age of sixteen, and anyone who looked closely could see the crippling effects of this. He was required to be on the machine for four to six hours, three times a week. Like any young person, he would sometimes rebel against the treatment, become seriously ill, and have to be admitted to the hospital. He came close to death more than once. Gradually, he adjusted to the treatment and used the time to read the Bible and pray, deepening his life in the Spirit. He came from a strong family of believers and felt a call to the ministry at a young age.

When I met him, he was not in good health, having been through a botched renal transplant. At lunch he asked if I might be able to help him as a doctor. I said I would do whatever I could for him, whenever he liked.

Not too long after our first meeting, he called from Baton Rouge. He said, "Listen, Doc, they're doing everything they can for me and they don't know what's wrong with me, and I'm dying. Can you help me? None of the doctors here in Louisiana can get this thing straight."

"Fly on out—get here as quickly as you can," I said.

When he arrived, I met him in the emergency room. I thought that his kidney problems might be causing complications with his heart and did an ultrasound study. His whole heart was full of fluid, and he was closer to death than anyone knew.

I ordered surgery immediately. Once the fluid was removed from his heart, he rebounded immediately and did great. I became his doctor, and he became one of my spiritual counselors. Subsequently, I found out that both David Hogan and Greg Rider had come out of Bethany World Prayer Center and been mentored by Joel's father and grandfather. I had always wondered who had influenced them, and now I knew.

In this way the Crandall family began to have a prayer team— people to intercede with us and back us up during the tough times. Deborah and I began flying occasionally to Baton Rouge to worship with Pastor Joel and others in the Bethany World Prayer Center community. I'd spend time with him discussing the Scriptures and what they say about healing.

This taught me, once again, that at the heart of Christian spirituality lies the principle of exchange. I became Joel's doctor, and he became my spiritual counselor. I now have relationships with many people like this: I help them physically, and they help me spiritually.

The Front Lines

One of the things I learned from Pastor Joel Stockstill, the Hunters, and others they introduced me to including Andrew and Randy McMillan—great charismatic missionaries in South America—is that God's blessing comes when a Christian accepts being on the front lines for God. The amazing stories of God's blessings they told all came from times when they put themselves at risk in God's service.

For example, Andrew and Randy McMillan were among the few North American missionaries who remained in Colombia—specifically Medellín—during guerrilla and terrorist attacks in the eighties and nineties. Andrew and Randy stayed, and God blessed them for it. I'm sure this was a deep influence on my thinking when I faced the hardest time of all in the days ahead.

Through this evolving prayer network, what our family was going through began to be known to a wider circle. This resulted in instances of spiritual generosity that were astounding. People started flying to the Palm Beach area just to pray with Chad. (Chad, incidentally, didn't enjoy the extra attention. To him it was a constant reminder of his disease.)

One day I received a call from a man in Oregon. He said, "I heard about your son. The Lord told me to fly out and pray for him."

"God did?"

"Yes, He did."

"When are you going to be here?"

"I'll be there in two days."

In two days the doorbell rang. The man from Oregon walked in. "I'm here to pray for your son," he said. "All I'll need is ten minutes."

We sat in the living room together with Chad and prayed for those ten minutes. At the end of this very brief time, the man said, "I've honored the Lord." And he left—just like that. He paid all of his expenses and never asked for anything in return.

Pastor César Castellanos pastors one of the fastest-growing churches in the world with more than 250,000 members at its Bogotá, Colombia, location alone.[1] Many think of Pastor Castellanos as the "Billy Graham of South America." Frankly, I had never heard of Pastor Castellanos when he called me one day at home. He said, "I've heard about your son, and I'm flying up tomorrow from Bogotá." He landed in Miami, drove to our house, and prayed with Chad for two hours. He told us, "There's a huge battle in the heavens over your son. Just keep praying. Ask as many people to join you as you can. There's a huge battle."

I wanted to extend him our hospitality after we had prayed together, but he said he had to return to Colombia immediately.

He drove straight back to Miami, boarded another plane, and arrived back in South America the same day. It was hard to realize: the Billy Graham of South America was here to pray with our son—he came all that way and went back the same day just to pray with Chad!

Blessings

Through these events we saw how lavishly God loved Chad and us. We began receiving similar blessings more often than we could count. The little house we owned where missionaries and other ministers stayed for short periods was particularly helpful, as these men and women of God would come to our house in the evenings for dinner and we'd sit and talk over how God had revealed Himself in their ministries. Their stories of miracles built up Chad's faith and his parents'.

Occasionally we'd have someone stay who was overly eager to see evidences of the supernatural, found the devil under every toadstool, and mistook yawning for the casting out of demons. But even those who had gone around the spiritual bend proved a blessing in one way or another. We knew they wanted God's will to prevail in our lives.

We continued to go to crusades, particularly those of Benny Hinn. I needed Benny's ministry during that time and found praying with him powerful.

We went to other healing services as well, whether they were in a church, a crusade, or a revival. Anything we could do to advance the kingdom of God in our lives, we did.

Sometimes we joked that our lives had become "tennis matches and God." We were on the road all the time. With each miracle service we attended, Chad seemed to get better. He certainly received a spiritual lift.

I also sought out the great evangelist Reinhard Bonnke, who talks about how Satan likes to enter a person's life wherever there's a weakness in his character or behavior or circumstances. We had certainly encountered this—without knowing it—in the case of the Togo fertility statue and Chad's infatuation with Peter Pan. Common weaknesses like alcohol abuse, drug addiction, pornography, and marital discord also provide openings to the devil's destructive ways. But it can even be something like a car accident or surgical trauma that makes someone vulnerable.

Prayer and Fasting

Many of the men and women of God with whom I've become close emphasize fasting along with prayer as a means of preparation for the tasks to which God calls us. I've found that if I fast and pray before a speaking engagement I feel the power of the Lord in a way I don't otherwise. I usually practice liquid fasts, drinking plenty of fluids but not eating anything solid. The first three days are rough, but then the body quiets and the mind and spirit are able to commune with God in a powerful way. As a means of honoring Chad and his struggle, we fasted frequently during his illness. When Chad faced particularly tough treatments, we would fast until he had endured the suffering the procedures entailed.

I realize now that Chad's illness taught me how to fight the spiritual battle every Christian faces. We have to cling to God through reading and meditating upon the Scriptures, through prayer and fasting, through radical obedience, and through joining together with other believers both for the sake of community and to accomplish tasks that are too big for any individual. I had been a Christian for twenty-five years without really understanding how to fight the battle.

I'll never forget getting slammed by the devil when I went into a situation unprepared. I knew I had God on my side, but there's a difference between godly confidence and presumption. Even the disciples were not able to cast out certain demons, which Jesus said demanded fasting and prayer.

Early in Chad's illness I went to New York, to the Hamptons on Long Island, to give a lecture on cardiology. We were scheduled to speak to a community group on preventive health care—particularly keeping the heart healthy. This event took place at a private school. The school was classified as "alternative," and a lot of actors and actresses as well as New York media moguls sent their children there. The place was stuffed with bamboo plants, African masks, and what looked to me like voodoo dolls. As soon as I arrived I felt a sense of oppression.

I went into the kitchen, waiting my turn to speak. One of the organizers waiting with me, not a Christian, commented that the place gave her the creeps—it felt evil. It certainly felt that way to me. I got riled up about the devil's presence, and I thought I'd take care of the matter.

When I went into the amphitheater to give my lecture, I said silently, *You devil, I'm going to get you. You have no right to do this. In the name of Jesus, leave this place.* As I began speaking, strange reverberations started bouncing off the walls, and the longer they went on the more they sounded like voices. The audience members looked around them. What was going on? Laughing and hissing seemed to be coming out of the walls.

I looked at the audiovisual technician, asking, "What's going on? Are we getting echoes from other rooms?"

He didn't know.

"Check it."

"Everything seems to be fine."

"Well, turn it off and let's see what happens."

He did, and the supernatural heckling continued.

I was really starting to be teed off then, and I prayed once more, "In the name of Jesus, I command you to stop!"

The voices stopped.

So I started my lecture. I was using a PowerPoint presentation, and the movie screen started going up and down uncontrollably. I looked at the audiovisual technician again. What was up? The hair on my arms stood up as I started freaking out.

I asked the technician to turn off the screen, but it continued to scroll up and down in fits and starts. Finally, I walked over and unplugged it and was able to finish my lecture. As soon as I did, I headed back to Florida. The place was too bizarre. I thought just getting out of there would put an end to the spiritual oppression.

The "Widow Maker"

When I arrived at the airport, I pulled my suitcase out of the backseat and felt a sharp pain in my shoulder. I couldn't understand how I might have pulled a muscle. I put the suitcase down, popped the handle, and rolled it into the airport. As I walked the pain intensified. I was only forty-eight, not diabetic, didn't smoke, with no family history of heart disease. It couldn't be my heart.

I boarded the plane and the pain went away. When I arrived in Palm Beach, I picked up my bag. Toting it brought back the pain in my shoulder, now with a little pressure in my chest. But I was fine again by the time I arrived home.

It was late fall and the kids wanted to go to the beach that night to hunt for sea turtles. That sounded like lots of fun. So we went to the north end of the island and Chad and Christian got out and were racing around with flashlights—this was early in Chad's battle with cancer, remember. I walked along in the sand or tried; I could not go twelve steps without getting a severe pain in my chest. It was as if I had run the 440 and I had that liver ache that makes you stop, only this was far more intense. The most unbelievable pain you could ever have. I would stop and rest, feel better, try to catch up with the kids, and then immediately feel the onset of pain once more. It didn't take long for me to sit down in the sand and rest. The kids raced by, saying, "What's wrong, Dad? Come on!"

"I had a hard day, I guess. You go on."

I watched them go down to the end of the beach, and as they turned to come back I wondered how I would make it back to the car. I didn't want to tell my wife. I kept going through a differential diagnosis sequence in my head, explaining to myself why it couldn't be heart disease.

At the end of the night I managed to make it back to the car. I drove home and the pain went away. I took a bunch of aspirin and went to bed, resolving to forget about the episode.

The next morning I felt fine. I thought what I experienced might have been a fluke or brought on by stress. But I decided to test it. My wife runs in the morning. I thought I'd walk along behind

Deborah. (If I collapsed she was sure to see me on her way back to the house.) But I didn't make it to the end of the driveway without severe pain. I sat on the steps and waited until she came back. I said, "Deborah, you have to take me to the hospital. I've got a heart problem. I don't know why, but I do."

As we were driving in, I called the hospital, telling them to get the operating room ready. I called my partner in our cardiology practice and told him to sterilize his instruments. He thought I was joking at first, but I managed to convince him with a description of my symptoms.

When we arrived at the hospital, Chad did not want to come in. He had been through too many treatments. Bad things would happen if he went into that place.

Deborah told Chad he had to come in. "This is your dad."

"I can't go in, Mom," he said, and started crying. "I can't make it through this, what I'm going through, without Dad."

Deborah said, "You have to come in, son. Dad is sick. We have to take care of him."

So he came in, but he was a bundle of nerves, worrying about me.

Deborah received permission to stand outside the operating room, and she pinned herself, spread-eagle, up against the operating room door while I was being worked on, crying out to God for my life, to spare me. That no harm would come to me.

The boys told her she was embarrassing them.

She did not care. "This is your dad's life! We have to cry out to God for him."

By the time the medical team had me on the table, I was screaming in pain. I had what's called the "widow-maker lesion." Three major arteries feed the heart, and the main one is called the

LAD: it runs down the middle of the heart and feeds the bulk of the muscle. The widow-maker lesion is a blockage, a stenosis, at the very beginning of the artery. It shuts off the whole arterial bed that feeds most of the heart, and it usually results in death. That's why that ache was so severe. The whole heart was crying out for blood and it couldn't get any—my LAD was 99 percent blocked. I had an emergency angioplasty and received two stents.

My partner put me in the intensive care unit overnight. The next day, I felt fantastic, and in the afternoon I pulled out the IVs, dressed, and prepared to leave. The nurses came running—"You can't do this." But, being rebellious, I insisted I was fine and left. (Doctors truly are the worst patients.)

I learned two things from this episode—lessons that appear to be contradictory but are actually a paradox that is the hallmark of everything I do. The first is that you have to be prepared to fight the spiritual battle. You cannot just invoke the name of Jesus as if waving a magic wand. When going into a new territory like the lecture venue, where oppressive forces might be present, you have to be prayed up and fasted up and have people interceding for you; otherwise, the devil will find weaknesses and exploit them to his advantage. As I sometimes tell people now, you have to prepare and think like a Green Beret or a Navy SEAL. You need to be in training every day, because you never know when the president—or the Lord—is going to call you into battle.

Part of that training, as with other types of soldiers, comes in the form of taking care of one's health. I had to get serious about exercise, stay on a restricted diet, get a periodic stress test, and pray for the healing of my body. The physical and the spiritual *go together*. I tell my patients, "I'm going to give you the best of modern medicine and the best of Jesus." Any weakness in one's spiritual or physical preparation for the battle we find ourselves fighting can be an entry point for evil—the "open door" Reinhard Bonnke talks about. I was prepared neither spiritually nor physically for what I faced on Long Island, and the devil nearly used my lack of preparation to take me out permanently.

Now I pray for healing in my body every day. "Lord, heal my heart; keep it strong so I can go the distance." I knew then that I had to stay in shape for my son, just as I know now that I have to stay in shape for the opportunities of service God presents, in both medicine and ministry.

I constantly tell people we have to stay in shape for our Savior so we can go the distance. I don't want you taken out at age fifty, because God's got a lot of work for you to do up until at least age seventy—the three score and ten the Bible indicates as a natural life span. I particularly hate to see young ministers taken out early, particularly if they haven't taken care of themselves; I consider this poor stewardship.

Hurricanes

If I had begun to understand *how* to fight the spiritual battle, I would soon need everything I had learned and more. Four months after the bone marrow transplant, Chad's leukemia came back. We were devastated.

His counts rose. He started losing weight again. And he developed a brain tumor behind his left ear. The tumor made him nauseated so that he could not eat, and he rapidly wasted away.

I admitted him to the hospital myself, stayed with him, and gave him more medicine, trying to restore his strength at least partially.

When we reached the point where we didn't know what else to do, we took him back to M. D. Anderson in September 2004. They told us of another experimental drug that was becoming available—BMS. They wanted to put Chad through another course of treatment.

After more chemo treatments, M. D. Anderson asked us to take Chad home and give him a series of treatments there to restore his strength. If we did that, we could bring Chad back to M. D. Anderson and they would put him on the new drug.

While Chad was undergoing treatment at the hospital in Palm Beach, hurricanes Frances and then Jeanne battered our area. Jeanne came ashore with winds up to 120 miles per hour and knocked out the power at the hospital—and two-thirds of the county. The hospital didn't have any water and the staff quickly ran out of food. Chad had to be moved out of his hospital room because a tree was smashing against his window. My wife stayed by him as I boarded up the house.

Chad wasn't doing well. His bone marrow was no longer functioning as the cumulative effects of the chemotherapy devastated his system. When the power went out at the hospital, although they had backup generators, the institution's ability to provide care was virtually knocked out, too. Deborah called me, frantic. Chad needed blood. The hospital could no longer supply the needed transfusion—the blood bank was empty. "There's no blood here!" Deborah screamed into the phone so that I could hear above the wind. "You have to get it. Chad will die unless you get him some blood."

"What about the emergency personnel at the hospital?"

"They won't go out in the storm. They say it's too dangerous. You'll have to do it!"

"Where am I going to get blood in the middle of a hurricane?"

"The blood bank in the north part of the county. Just go up I-95."

In the midst of a hurricane? "All right," I said. "You're sure this is critical?"

"Chauncey, your son is *dying*. How clear do I have to make this?"

"I'll go. I'm gone."

I couldn't leave Christian behind, so I told him, "Strap yourself in, son. We're going to get blood for your brother."

The 100 mph winds felt as if they would topple our Range Rover at any moment. I put it in low gear and drove at a snail's pace to keep it from being lifted off the road. There were no other cars. The only power lines we could see were on the ground. At midafternoon the world was a gray blur of wind and rain.

When I finally made it to the blood bank, I banged on the door to be let inside. "Open up. I need your help!" I went to every window and rapped. I saw someone look back finally. He looked so startled he might have been seeing the storm come in. I motioned frantically for him to open the door.

He finally cracked the door open. "What do you need, man? What's going on?"

"I need blood for my son. I'm a doctor. I need blood. He's type O negative. I have to rush it to Saint Mary's Hospital to save his life."

He let me inside finally. "Man, the electricity is off. I don't know how—I don't think we can do this."

"I don't care how you do it. Just do it. We need to get it to him today. Now. Right now."

"You came through the storm?"

"*Now!*"

He led me back to the cooler. He turned on the generator and the building's lights popped on. He found bags of blood that were properly matched and coded and put these in a cardboard box.

I went back to Christian, who was still in the car. I handed him the precious box of blood. "This is for your brother," I said. "Put your seat belt on."

All I could do was drive and pray. "God, protect us, because this is Chad's only hope." We made what would normally be a fifteen-minute trip in two hours, but we arrived in time.

CHAPTER 9

A Black Cloud and Lightning

The blood transfusions staved off Chad's death, but he remained in serious condition, his marrow not producing cells, his body wasting away. I had taken him through the full course of treatment recommended by M. D. Anderson, done everything they'd asked in order to try another experimental drug, BMS. So I called the hospital and made arrangements to bring Chad back in the fall of 2004.

Once in Houston, Chad went through an assessment and his supervising physician called me in for a conference.

"Dr. Crandall," he said, "I'm afraid your son hasn't shown the improvement we need."

I'm attuned to "doctor speak" and understood immediately where the conversation was heading. "I've done everything you wanted me to do," I said.

"I'm sure you have. But your son's too sick for an experimental treatment. It would skew the results of the trial."

"Listen, *Chief,* you told me what to do. We put him through it all. My son's life is on the line. He needs what you promised—BMS. I don't care about what's in your interests or the pharmaceutical company's. I don't care about the government's protocols and criteria, either. I fought through two hurricanes to get that boy a blood transfusion. And I'll do whatever it takes now to get him that drug."

"Dr. Crandall, he's too sick."

I jumped out of my seat and grabbed the lapels of his lab coat. *"My son is going to live!* You give him the drug. You've got a child. You know what it means to have a son. I need my boy! I need him to live!"

They finally gave him BMS. Within hours, he looked better. BMS attacked the mutated line of cells that Gleevec couldn't touch.

But BMS worked for only two weeks. Chad developed a rare mutation—the only one known to elude every available drug.

There was a third drug that could possibly bring about some improvement, although its effectiveness was speculative at best. But I pleaded once more for this drug to be administered.

We had to wait and wait some more to be put on the list for this third drug. The hospital gave Chad blood and platelets, and he was in and out of the hospital every three days. It was grueling.

Chad was so weak, he couldn't even talk. I'd wheel him around in the wheelchair. Nearly all his hair was gone. We would pass people standing by their IV poles, many grotesquely disfigured, their heads misshapen, their ears missing, their arms amputated as a result of cancer and its brutalizing treatments. No matter how often the halls were cleaned and disinfected, the ward smelled of decaying flesh.

As I've mentioned, treating patients in extremis is hard on everyone involved, and the worse Chad's condition became, the slower and less responsive the staff seemed to be. (Of course, Deborah and I were so desperate, the passing of time slowed almost to a stop.) But it's a fact that some days we had to wait six hours to see a doctor.

The hospital eventually administered the third experimental drug, but it did not work. Chad was now in God's hands, as he always had been, but in a way that was beyond anything but supernatural hope.

The Peace of Jesus

Chad's own spiritual journey during his illness was more concealed from us as his parents than we had realized. After he got over the initial embarrassment of being prayed for at evangelistic events and healing services, he took them in stride, but he largely kept his own counsel about what he experienced. When Deborah would press him about what he thought about César Castellanos's or Joel Stockstill's praying for him, he'd beg off. "Mom, if I tell you, you'll tell your friends, and then it will be all over town."

That didn't keep him from enjoying charismatic programs like *The 700 Club* and Kenneth Copeland's show. He'd pay particular attention when Pat Robertson or Kenneth Copeland would pray for people, hoping his own name would be mentioned. He remained well behaved even as he moved into adolescence. When a TV show came on that looked good then became too sexually explicit, he'd turn it off.

Chad was more theologically astute than his parents realized, too. This came out in a funny way when Deborah turned on a regular show in which a teacher of the Word emphasized prophecy. Deborah found pondering Christ's coming again a source of hope. But Chad protested, "Mom, we're not going to watch this. Nobody knows the end times."

Chad thought not only of himself but of his parents and his brother. He would say, "I'm sorry that I've ruined your life." That broke our hearts, and it was impossible to explain how infinitely richer Chad had made our lives.

As anyone facing death does, Chad wanted to know that he was right with God. Before we returned to Houston, Chad worried aloud that he was going to stand before God and there would be something he hadn't confessed or done. He knew that his salvation was from Christ alone, and yet he worried about going to heaven. Deborah kept telling him that this was the devil taunting and lying to him. His fears were sometimes prompted by the deaths of public figures. When Ray Charles and others died, Chad worried for days about whether they had gone to heaven.

Between treatments in Houston, Deborah would sometimes take Chad at night for car rides—to get him, if only for a while, as far away from the hospital environment as possible. Chad knew enough about his illness to understand that he was in trouble as never before. He could not avoid this knowledge, as he had contracted pneumonia and breathing became increasingly difficult. He had been asking us to explain his condition to him with a new urgency. In these circumstances, Deborah asked Chad if he felt there was anything more they needed to discuss, trying to draw out and assuage any fears that remained.

Chad said, "No, Mom, I've done everything. I've thought of everything. I've done my best."

"I have fought a good fight, I have finished my course" (2 Tim. 4:7 KJV)—that's how the apostle Paul put it, possibly with more elegance but not a smidgen more truth.

As I wheeled Chad around the hospital, from his bed to one treatment after another and back again, I caught him whispering something.

"What, Chad? What are you saying?"

"Dad, the peace of Jesus. The peace of Jesus."

"The peace of Jesus?"

"The peace of Jesus."

I've thought a lot about his saying this since, and I don't think "the peace of Jesus" was so much his own prayer—although it was that—as a blessing he wanted to extend to the hospital and especially the other patients. He wanted the peace of Jesus to descend on that hospital as it filled his heart. We had been told that a war in the heavenlies was being fought over Chad—a war in which Chad, not his father, was the chief protagonist. Deborah and I think the Holy Spirit prepared Chad for his death and gave him an unusual participation in the life of God even as he was passing from this life.

Chad, evidently when his parents weren't looking, read the Bible deeply and closely, with a prayerful attention spurred by his illness. Later we found his Bible had been underlined and annotated, passage after passage, especially those that had to do with fighting the spiritual battle. He seems to have especially liked Matthew 24:13: "He who stands firm to the end will be saved." And "Be on your guard; stand firm in the faith; be men of courage; be strong" (1 Cor. 16:13).

Spiraling Down

Deborah and I both were with Chad every moment from late August through the end of September 2004. At that point I had to return to my practice and work enough to pay the bills. I called nightly to find out how Chad was doing. The doctor kept saying he was doing well.

When I returned I didn't like what I found. Chad's pneumonia was much worse; he was suffering from malnutrition and bedsores—problems that should have been addressed with greater care. This is basic medicine, but it's medicine that often breaks down toward the end of someone's life because the personnel around the patient give up hope. Chad couldn't sleep at night because there was too much fluid in his lungs. All he could do was doze in a chair.

I'm ashamed to say I partly blamed Deborah for his condition. "Can't you see what's been happening?" I asked. "You should know better than to trust these people." In a situation like this the urge to blame someone becomes overwhelming. While I blamed her for the bad turn he'd taken, Deborah blamed me for Chad's being sick. Neither of us was at fault; the disease was at fault and was beating up our marriage in the bargain. Deborah was doing everything she could to keep him alive, preparing special foods and coaxing him with pleas of "Please eat!" I was trying everything I knew as a physician. We were constantly crying to God, "Heal him!" Nothing was working, and by this time we felt burned-out and almost numb.

I ordered oxygen and the people at the hospital were slow to respond. I thought I could do the simple remedial treatments that were necessary back at our apartment, so we took Chad home for about a week.

Toward the end of October Chad could hardly breathe one night, and we had to rush him back to the hospital. Once we put him in a hospital bed, Chad perked up somewhat. The doctor on duty that night recommended, nevertheless, that he be transferred from the general ward to the intensive care unit. Chad's X-rays revealed he had significant fluid in his lungs—he was drowning inside.

The doctor asked, "What do you want to do?"

"What in the world does that mean?"

"His lungs look terrible, Dr. Crandall. He's dying."

"Yes, and I don't want him to. *Isn't that the point?* He's got fluid in his lungs. That can be taken care of. In fact, it *should* have been taken care of. I was gone for a week to take care of my own practice. If Chad wasn't doing fine, someone should have told me."

"Let's get him into the ICU, as I've recommended, and get him feeling better. We can put him on a ventilator to help him breathe."

The mention of a ventilator nearly crushed the life out of me. They would put him on a ventilator and sedate him and he'd never open his eyes again. I'd never hear his voice again. He'd never respond to my hand squeeze again.

I said, "No ventilator. You can do whatever else you want—but no ventilator." On previous occasions I had already seen the ICU packed with kids on ventilators, their families weeping, their kids growing closer to death every minute. I still felt strongly that God was going to intervene and we were going to ride this thing out. I didn't want that chance cut short.

Chad was taken to the ICU. He was not put on a ventilator. Instead, to aid his breathing the doctor used a CPAP (continuous positive airway pressure) machine, which uses a special mask that pushes air in and out of the lungs, but without the aid of a breathing tube. There was no need to sedate Chad with the CPAP machine. Chad began to do better. His condition improved markedly, but it was still a battle.

A Mother's Miracle

In the last week of October, Chad's blood pressure dropped, his heart almost flatlined, and his whole body went limp. He was gone. His medical team came rushing into the room. Deborah scooped Chad up in her arms and sat him up in bed and held him upright. She started praying, repeating Bible verses over and over, the phrases spilling out, words rushing forward like a river. Scripture after Scripture flowed out, all long ago memorized from Dodie Osteen's book and others. I couldn't believe she had memorized so much or could have the stamina to pray and pray and pray in the face of her child's death.

One of Chad's nurses fell to her knees crying, acknowledging the presence of God. The respiratory tech was there, his eyes wide. I can't say a beam of light shone on Deborah and Chad, but it seemed as if it did. Deborah was speaking God and glory over her boy who was dead. The river of God's Word kept flowing. Deborah embraced Chad and God embraced Deborah and Chad came back to life. His body became pink—rosy with health.

The nurse said she had never seen anything like it. The respiratory tech said *he'd* never seen anything like it. "You prayed over your boy and he's alive," he said in wonder.

Deborah laid him back in bed. His skin color had not only

come back, but one of his major wounds had even healed. He had had a tumor on his side, and the skin there looked like a swirl of melted cheese from radiation and scar tissue. That place on his side looked as healthy and new now as a child's skin. It was as if God had literally touched him. His vital signs started coming up. And his breathing improved. Even his blood work returned to normal. We thought, *Wow, we've got a victory! He's going to make it!*

The following morning Deborah asked, "Chad, can you hear me? I love you."

He squeezed her hand and said, "I love you, too, Mom."

A Fight in the Heavenlies

But that day Chad's condition slipped again. The next day it was Halloween. We felt as if we were fighting the darkness all day. Nurses dressed as witches and techs as warlocks pranced around hanging fake cobwebs and taping up spiders. They were giggling and laughing and inadvertently collaborating with the darkness we were battling.

Deborah and I stayed with Chad all through the night. Christian was there, too. We had a telephone call from Larry Stockstill—Joel Stockstill's father—who recommended that we do what the Stockstills had done when Joel was near death one time. He advised us to stand over Chad and release him into the Lord's care. So I stood on one side of Chad's bed, and Deborah and Christian on the other, and we joined hands over Chad, making an arc of love and protection, and gave Chad's life into God's hands. We asked aloud for His will to be done in Chad's life (which both Deborah and I reminded the Lord was to heal him).

That night Deborah continued praying over Chad in silence. She heard God say to her, "Lift your praises to Me." So she did. "You are the Alpha and the Omega, the beginning and the end. I praise You, God." As long as she praised the Lord, Chad's vital signs were stable—his blood pressure remained normal, his heart rate steady. When she grew weary she was startled back to wakefulness by the monitor's warning beeps. She felt like Moses during the battle with the Amalekites described in Exodus 17. At God's direction, Moses stood on a hill overlooking the battle. As long as Moses held up his hands as he watched the battle, the Israelites prevailed. But when his hands dropped, the Amalekites began winning. Aaron and Hur finally helped him keep his arms up and the Israelites won the day. But Deborah didn't have her Aaron and Hur. I tried my best to support her, as did Christian, but we fell asleep sometime after midnight. Deborah prayed until three thirty when she felt if she could only close her eyes for a moment, she could begin again. But then sleep overcame her as well.

This experience taught her of God's power—how the fight was going on in the heavenlies. She believes that Chad was fighting, too, and, as we subsequently were to learn, he made a final choice.

The next morning dawned with a bright blue sky—November 1, All Saints' Day. I felt tired and beat-up from the long night but cheered by the start of a new day. I stood at the window, and off in the distance I saw a small dark cloud in the middle of bright blue sky. There were no other clouds in the sky. But this black cloud was coming straight toward us. I saw thunderbolts shooting out of it. I motioned to Deborah to come stand beside me, saying, "You're not going to believe this." There were scores of blackbirds in the trees below us. And that cloud kept coming.

I immediately thought, as did she, *Not today, Lord, not today.* We were afraid that the black cloud with its thunderbolts was God in his Shechinah glory coming to take Chad to heaven. I kept thinking, *I don't want this to be the day. This isn't You, Lord, is it? Not today. I need him.*

I went to Chad's bedside and sat with him, but all the time I was watching that cloud come closer. The closer it came, the more Chad's breathing slowed down. More quickly than I expected, the cloud was right over the building, lightning glazed the windows, thunder shook the building, and rain poured down. Chad's heart rate dropped. He struggled for another breath or two, his chest heaving upward.

Not today! Not now! I really need this child. He's got a brother who needs him. He has a call on his life. I need him.

He took his last breath—the monitor's beeper went off. The heart monitor's line went flat and stayed that way.

"I Will Run to You, God"

I was so far into grief that Deborah's reaction could not have been more astonishing. "Do you feel the peace?" she asked.

"No, I don't feel the peace," I said, angry.

Deborah was walking around the room.

"I feel it," Christian said. "It's so nice. It's unbelievable."

All I could do was pray, "God, I've done everything You've asked of me. *Give me back my son! My heart is breaking!*"

There was only silence and Chad's lifeless body in my arms.

I knew I had a decision to make, right then, at my son's death-bed. "I don't understand what's happened," I told God. "Either I'll run to You now and give You absolutely everything in my life from this moment on or I'm going to abandon You, as I feel abandoned. I'm mad and I don't like You anymore. What should I do? What can I do?"

I realized then that during those four years I had experienced too much of God to abandon Him; I knew too much of His reality, even if I could not fathom His purpose in allowing Chad's death.

"I will run *to You*, God," I declared. "For the rest of my life, with all my heart, mind, and soul. But if I run to You, Lord, I want a million souls for Your kingdom in exchange for my son. I plant the martyr's seed, Lord, because he has been martyred by evil and disease."

I laid Chad back in bed. Deborah arranged his body under the covers and tucked him in. I told Deborah, "I've made my decision. I will follow the Lord. But it says in my Bible that we can pray to raise the dead, in Jesus' name. I would like for us to pray together for Chad to be raised. I've already made my decision to choose obedience, whatever God decides to do. But I want to act on what God allows us to do."

We had a bottle of anointing oil, and Deborah, Christian, and I anointed Chad's body for the next hour and a half, crying out to God. "Bring him back, Jesus. Raise him up from the dead, Lord. You are a great and almighty God. You can do this." As we anointed Chad, I realized the truth of what the Scriptures teach—we are but clay. Chad's flesh no longer had the resilience of life; everywhere I touched him his flesh showed the marks. Deborah shut his lips and they stayed closed, like clay, dust.

After all of our prayers, I said, "It's done. Let's go home."

The next day during her prayer time Deborah was given a message from God: "Remember Stephen." She didn't know what this meant. Later, as we thought about it, we realized that Stephen was the first martyr and that his death and the threat of further persecution caused many of the new Christians to leave Jerusalem and spread the gospel across the Mediterranean world. Was this a promise that my son's death would be honored with the one million souls for which I had asked?

CHAPTER 10

Home-Going

Chad's funeral took place at the Royal Poinciana Chapel in Palm Beach. After the battle we had been through, I did not want a minister to conduct the service—someone who would speak with us for a half hour and then devise a well-meaning but superficial service. We decided upon a "home-going service," as we called it. We were grieving and grief cannot and should not be denied. At the same time, Chad's struggle had shown us God's power and God's glory, and we wanted people to understand the true character of God as the One who brings life—not death. "Let's have a victory message in this," I said. "Let's win the Island of Palm Beach to Christ!"

I knew that out of respect for our family many people would come. I did not expect the church to be packed to overflowing.

In the end, we did have a minister officiate—Deborah's brother, Pastor Don Newell. I spoke as well. What people remembered most, though, were Deborah's remarks.

She began by saying, "I want to first thank everyone for all your prayers, love, and support. I want you to know that your prayers did not go unanswered."

Didn't they? I imagine many at the funeral or those reading this would take Deborah's words as merely the pious sentiment of a mother desperately trying to compensate for her loss. We do not believe it when people say things like this, but we allow them their comfort. Chad died. He was not healed of leukemia as so many had prayed.

But such a "realistic" view is real only if we think in terms of our natural desires and the time given to us, not God's will and eternity. Deborah recounted several of the remissions Chad had been blessed with through prayer and medicine. Then she spoke of Chad's passing, and through her prayerful intuition she saw, prophetically and through faith, a greater reality than we wanted to envision and one that we later had even more reason to embrace. She spoke of the night when the words of Scripture flowed from her like a river and Chad came back to life before our eyes. Then she said: "We had Christian nurses and a respiratory therapist rejoicing, because they had never seen anything like this before. But there was something different now. Chad had seen heaven and felt the Father's love. Jesus had embraced him, and Chad knew the overwhelming love of his Savior."

She then spoke of Chad's passing—the peace both Christian and she felt and yet her desire to keep Chad with us. "Chad," she had said that day, "I know you're standing with Jesus. We can feel it. But I'm going to ask God to bring you back again." But Chad had had enough, as Deborah recounted. He wanted to stay in paradise with Jesus.

"I believe Chad was healed when he entered heaven," Deborah said. "His prayers and our prayers were answered. Hebrews 13:8

says, 'Jesus Christ is the same yesterday and today and forever.' In Revelation 21 [v. 4] we read: 'And God shall wipe away all tears from their eyes'—Chad's eyes—'and there shall be no more death, neither sorrow, nor crying, neither shall there be any more pain: for the former things are passed away' [KJV]. May the grace of our Lord Jesus Christ be with you. Amen."

Comforts

After the service, we learned that Chad must have been watching over the banisters of heaven, smiling with approval as people came into the kingdom as a direct result of his life and death. One was a lifeguard. We had lifeguards from our club as ushers, because they were always watching over Chad and Christian. Lifeguarding in Palm Beach is a career—this man was still fit and trim but in his sixties. After the service, he stopped a friend of ours and said, "I've never experienced anything like this before." He told us subsequently that he had accepted Christ as Savior.

The next day, the father of a family well known in Palm Beach society called a friend of ours. "I need to tell you something," he said. "We just want you to tell the Crandalls that Chad did not die in vain. After that service, my wife and I were up all night crying, and we recommitted our lives to Christ. They need to know that!"

A Jewish woman took one of Deborah's friends aside and asked her, "How did she do that? How did she get up there and speak of her son without crying?"

Deborah's friend said, "Because she knows her God. She has a personal relationship with Christ, and that's how she was able to do it."

The next week another woman stopped Deborah on the bike trail and asked, "Will you teach me the Bible? You have something I don't have, and I need to learn about it from you."

Such requests were multiplied many times over, and now Deborah, despite her shyness, is leading a booming Bible study. God equips those He calls.

A Message in the Sky

We had a natural need for comfort, though, too. While God has assured our ultimate victory over death in Jesus, God doesn't demand that we deny our suffering. Jesus came in the flesh and suffered Himself—that's the meaning of the Cross. Through the Cross He asks us not to run away from Him but to run to Him in our grief and fear. He asks us to unite our suffering with His—or as the apostle Paul wrote, to "fill up in my flesh what is still lacking in regard to Christ's afflictions, for the sake of his body, which is the church" (Col.1:24). Paul even went so far as to say, "I want to know Christ and the power of his resurrection and the fellowship of sharing in his sufferings, becoming like him in his death" (Phil. 3:10).

God comforted us in our grief in remarkable ways, two of which stand out. One of the most painful experiences is that the person whose loss is being grieved is no longer there to communicate with. Deborah and I longed for just one more opportunity to embrace Chad and tell him we loved him. We wondered if he would know anything of our lives in the future—whether on the day we went to heaven Chad would recognize us as his parents. Deborah read the wonderful book *Heaven* by Randy Alcorn. Alcorn cites the passage from Revelation in which the martyrs in heaven ask the Lord when God will avenge their blood. The writer asks the question, "If the martyrs understand that their deaths have not been made right, what more do they know of earthly events?" Many Christians believe that the company of heaven—that "great cloud of witnesses"—not only witnesses to God's glory but also witnesses human history, including the lives of those with whom they were close.

One night as Deborah, Christian, and I were walking on the bike trail with the dogs, Deborah stopped in the middle of the trail, raised her hands to heaven, and prayed aloud, "Oh, God, is Chad still aware of us down here?" I was trying to get in as much exercise as possible and had walked ahead, but Christian was standing by his mother's side. Deborah looked into the sky to her right and saw YES in the cloudlike letters a skywriter would make.

She asked Christian if he saw what she saw.

"Yeah, Mom."

"Did you hear—"

"Yeah, I heard what you prayed. That's *amazing*!"

"But where's the skywriter?"

A private pilot carried on a ministry of skywriting in the Palm Beach area. Many days as Christian and Chad would be playing tennis or swimming at the club, we'd look up and see "God loves you" or "Jesus loves you" written by this pilot. But on that day they could not see the plane or hear it.

"Where's the skywriter, Christian?"

"I don't know, but Mom, it says Yes!"

Deborah and Christian called to me to come running, which I did. But by the time I reached them and looked where they were pointing, I couldn't see anything. The letters had come and gone.

This remained a huge comfort to Deborah. She confesses to

being "the type who needs a billboard sometimes," as we all do, and it was as if God had answered her prayer with a billboard in the sky.

I had my own confirmation of Chad's presence with the Lord. During our time at M. D. Anderson, we often attended Lakewood Church, where Joel Osteen is pastor. One of their associate ministers, Steve, came to pray with us regularly, relieving the spiritual loneliness we felt at first. A year later, I was invited to a Houston TV station to tape a segment about Jeff Markin being raised from the dead. I pulled my car into a parking space and immediately another car pulled in next to me. It was Steve.

Steve was so glad to see me, he said. He had to tell me something! Steve's mother, an elderly woman in her eighties, had a powerful ministry of intercessory prayer. At Steve's urging, she had been in prayer for Chad during the final weeks of his illness. Steve had been in the hospital the day of Chad's passing. He hadn't come into the room that day, but he had heard of Chad's passing.

Later that day, his mother called him. She had seen a vision of Chad, dressed in white sports clothes—like a tennis player—sitting on a mountain overlook, on a smooth round boulder. Although she did not know this, the Crandall family often went hiking in the Virginia mountains. The locale and Chad's attire provided details about his life that she probably had no way of knowing, which added credence to her vision. Steve's mother said, "I saw the boy you've been praying for. He was talking with the Lord. The Lord asked him what he wanted to do. Did he want to come home with the Lord or go back?" In her vision, Chad was at peace, full of joy. The Lord told him it was his choice. If he wanted to resume his life, he could, or he could come to paradise with God. The mother told Steve, "Chad said he wanted to go with the Lord."

Steve said, "Mom, you don't know this, but Chad just left. He's with the Lord now."

She said, "Oh, son, I've been praying so hard for him." Evidently, Steve's mother received this vision a few hours before Chad died.

Our Share in the Cross

As I thought over the next weeks and months about losing Chad, I realized that Deborah, Christian, and I were the ones still suffering from his loss. Chad was with the Lord. He was in glory, happy. He wasn't feeling the terrible pain anymore. I became grateful, in a sense, for the ultimate healing that God had brought about in Chad's life through his death. The Scriptures tell us: "No matter how many promises God has made, they are 'Yes' in Christ. And so through him the 'Amen' is spoken by us to the glory of God" (2 Cor. 1:20).

I'm also beginning to realize that through Chad's death, Christ gave the Crandall family a share in Christ's cross. An opportunity to join our suffering to Christ's for the conversion of souls and the life of the world. When people ask me now why God should be using us as He is, I come back to that fundamental decision I made at Chad's deathbed: to run to God instead of away from Him. To accept the cross of Christ as part of my reality. "With his stripes we are healed," the Scriptures tell us (Isa. 53:5 KJV). And 1 Peter 4:12–19 says we are *privileged* to share in Christ's suffering.

The Cross is a gift that nobody really wants. It's the gift that people almost always turn away from, choosing to curse God rather than submit to God's will. Even Jesus Himself sweated drops of blood contemplating the agony of His coming death. But Christ's willingness to die—and our willingness to die with Him—is the source of resurrection power. I believe that God began blessing me as He never had before, because in my own hour of feeling abandoned by God, in that moment when I came as near as I could to understanding what Jesus felt when He cried, "My God, my God, why have you forsaken me?" (Matt. 27:46), I claimed God as *my God.*

From that moment on I knew that my life in the flesh—in terms of most worldly desires, at least—was over. I was here for only one reason: to serve our almighty God and Lord, Jesus Christ.

In return God seemed to say to me: "Now I'm going to use you. You've been broken, and yet you haven't turned from Me; you've turned to Me. Now I will use you to advance the kingdom of God."

Shortly afterward—and I can only describe it this way—the heavens opened.

CHAPTER 11

The Heavens Open

After Chad passed, our friends the Hunters asked me to speak at a healing service at Victory Christian Center Church in the north Houston suburb of Kingwood. I had presented papers at medical conferences but otherwise had never done much public speaking. I spoke at the church about how I had run after God for the past four years and the works of healing I had seen in Mexico and elsewhere.

Many in the meeting were moved, wanted to hear more, and crowded around me after the service. It was an odd feeling being in that position for the first time—a public figure through whom the Holy Spirit had touched others. I wanted to say, "Hey, I'm no one. I'm just a doctor. I don't have anything you can't have. I ran after the Lord."

Then I realized that while this was true, our family's experience had led to one of life's deepest griefs—the loss of a child—and in

140

the end, I hadn't blamed God. That's what most people do, and I fully understand the impulse. Remaining loyal to God gave me a deeper understanding of how God looks at life. Because God and I—if I can be permitted to say this—shared in common the loss of a son. I had participated, on a human level, in the mystery that is making for the final restoration of heaven and earth. It was as if God were saying to me, "Do you understand now what I suffered when I gave My Son for the life of the world? Do you understand what I continue to suffer as people fail to comprehend My love? In being broken you have come to a new understanding of these things."

Shortly afterward, I was invited by the missionary evangelist Andrew McMillan to Colombia, South America, to speak at a men's conference. I spoke on Friday morning to about 250 men, and Andrew liked what he heard so much that he invited me to speak that night to a young people's gathering of 1,500. The event took place in a gymnasium, and a couple of *barranquilla* bands warmed up the kids with their happy Latin rhythms.

I had never spoken to a crowd that large, and as Andrew had suggested I might minister beside him at the service's end—praying for the Holy Ghost to fall on individuals and work healings—I wondered what was in store. By then I had seen many people slain in the Spirit and had even been blown backward by the Spirit the first time David Hogan prayed for Chad's healing, but I had never seen anyone slain in the Spirit as the result of my own prayers.

As I was preaching to the young people, I started talking about boldness. We should be bold in Christ. Even young people should be bold in Christ. "Go out and minister to other youth," I told the young crowd. "Minister to your parents and your neighborhoods.

You can have this boldness if you ask for it in Jesus' name. If you'd like to be bold in Christ, I will pray for you to receive this gift. Who wants the courage and freedom in expressing your beliefs that only Christ can give? Are there fifteen here who want it?"

Fifteen young people came out of the crowd and lined up on the platform behind me. I walked toward the young man who was first in the lineup on the left and before I was halfway to him, I held up my hand to pray for the blessing of boldness to fall on him and he fell backward, slain in the Spirit. I did not feel anything myself. But it was as though I had a force field around me, because with my next steps toward the second in line, he went down. Then the third, the fourth. These weren't "courtesy drops," as one sometimes sees at Pentecostal meetings. These teenagers went *out*. (In a peaceful way—the falling of the Holy Ghost usually brings a profound peace.) Every person in that line went over peacefully until I reached the fifteenth. He fell over, but then he started manifesting demons, writhing and slithering on the ground, growling, yelling, and screaming. I bent down to him and commanded the demons to come out in Jesus' name.

My host, Andrew McMillan, came over and said, "Listen, man, I don't know what is going on here, but I want you to pray for every young person here tonight. It's like you are in a Holy Ghost bubble."

Inside the "Holy Ghost Bubble"

The young people had already started lining up in front of the platform—once they saw the first fifteen slain, the whole crowd wanted the same blessing. So I went into the crowd and held my

hand up to pray and everyone hit the ground, toppling like domi-
noes. One in fifty would start manifesting demons, and Andrew
and I would pray over them, calling on Jesus to free those suffering
spiritual oppression from their bondage. By the end of a long, long
night, fifteen hundred young people had received a special blessing of the Holy Spirit.

Andrew McMillan has been a faithful missionary in Colombia
for many years. He has been a leader in the Pentecostal and charismatic revival that has swept through Colombia and other Latin
American nations. As we had a moment to ourselves after the service, he told me, "I've never seen anything like this. God is all over
you, man. This is incredible."

"Andrew, I don't know what this is exactly. I'm just doing what
I've been asked."

"You have to do the Sunday service tomorrow," he said. "Will
you?"

I quickly agreed.

As we were preparing to go back to Andrew's house that
evening, a young woman told us of what had happened in her
life that night. She had been passing by on the street, and she felt
God's power and was drawn into the service. She had been on her
way to commit suicide by throwing herself in front of a bus. She
was not a member of Andrew McMillan's church. She simply felt
the power of God drawing her away from destruction and toward
Him. Instead of committing suicide, she gave her life to Christ that
night.

The next day, I started preaching and ministering again, with
Andrew translating. There were thirty-six hundred people present
and the same thing happened—the same blessing of the Holy
Spirit. We called a couple of people up onto the platform, and they

were slain in the Spirit. Then I went into the congregation, and everyone I prayed for was slain in the Spirit. Imagine praying for more than three thousand people, one by one. Sometimes I was running from one end of the room to the other, just touching people's heads, and each and every one received the blessing. It was unbelievable. The more so to me, I imagine, because I didn't feel anything. Sometimes ministers will speak of feeling God's presence as heat or a warm tingling, but I didn't feel anything. I knew that whatever was happening was all God, not me. But I was not only willing but thrilled to obey God's leading. I went from row to row, sometimes climbing over chairs to reach people, and the Holy Ghost gave everyone the gift of resting in God.

There was another service that night, with the same number of people, and the same thing happened.

Andrew claims he still hasn't witnessed a similar move of God, ever. He told me that my medical practice was important, my essential identity as a doctor should not change, but he implored me to keep ministering. "You have to keep this going."

"You're Out of Control!"

At home, I found myself worn-out from having prayed for so many people individually. I quickly came to understand how connected the physical and the spiritual are. "Lord, if You are going to use me like this," I said in my prayers, "I have to get stronger."

Many evangelists and missionaries, like David Hogan, are into physical fitness for just this reason. Though I had begun taking better care of myself following the angioplasty, I intensified my health care regime at this time. I joined a gym, started working out regularly, and began eating right. I started practicing what I so often tell ministers who come to me as a doctor now—it's important as God's servants to honor the body as God's temple. Otherwise, we give the devil an easy opportunity to shorten our service to God, and that's not being properly grateful for the gift of God's calling. There's a reason the apostle Paul compared the spiritual life to a race, and I wonder if the apostle had the marathon in mind.

I wonder whether God seems so sparing with His gifts at times because few of us have any idea how prepared we must be to receive and nurture them. God's gifts may often appear more as burdens—heavy ones—than pleasures. God's using me in new ways eventually challenged Deborah and our marriage.

When I came home from Colombia, I told Deborah what had happened. She thought my stories were great, but she received them a little bit as one receives the tales of derring-do told by a child. She half suspected that I was weaving my own legends.

After Colombia, the invitations for me to speak arrived weekly. I could only accept the invitations that allowed me six-week intervals between travels, otherwise I could never have continued my medical practice. For the first eighteen months of my new life as a lay minister, I traveled alone, and Deborah was never an eyewitness to how the Holy Spirit was ministering through me. She was concentrating on catching up with our son, Christian, whose need for parenting and especially his mother's presence was great after all the attention we had paid to Chad.

Then I spoke to a big youth event at Joel Stockstill's church, Bethany World Prayer Center, and Deborah came with me. There were six thousand young people and senior ministers from around the Baton Rouge area and far beyond in attendance. At the end of the service, all the pastors were called to the platform to pray individually with young people, and Joel asked me to come up and pray as well.

I started praying one by one with teenagers and they started dropping, one after another. This frightened Deborah. When I pray for people, I feel emboldened by the Spirit, and I tend to shout. Deborah started tugging at me, telling me to keep my voice down, not to put my hands on anyone's forehead—she wanted me to stop ministering. Having never seen anything like this happen through me, she wondered whether the kids falling backward might get hurt. She was concerned.

Then I began praying for a girl who started manifesting demons, growling and screaming. Her sister was standing by her side, frightened. Deborah reached over my shoulder and grabbed my hand. "I don't want you touching anyone else," she said.

I talked to the other ministers and asked them to continue praying with the girl who was manifesting demons, and then I went to pray for other teenagers.

Later, one of the ministers who began praying with the girl manifesting demons told me the rest of the story. She had been tortured by demons for years. Her grandmother, who was a charismatic believer, had cast out two demons from her, but the grandmother confessed to being unable to cast out a third. "Dr. Crandall," the minister told me, "you were able to cast out the third demon. She walked out of here set free!"

When we returned home, Deborah renewed her concerns. "I don't know what you've been doing, but I've never seen anything like that. You're out of control!"

"Deborah, I told you about Colombia. Did you think I was lying?"

"I don't care. This is just nuts. I don't know if you should be doing this."

I said, "Deborah, are you really going to put me in the position of choosing between you and God? After what we've been through? *Really?* I don't want this. The Lord has given this to me. I'm not worthy of it, but when I pray for people and this happens, we just have to go with the Holy Spirit."

"I don't *understand* it. I've never seen this from you and I've known you your whole life. From other people, yes, but not with you, and it frightens me."

I was about to make another rebuttal when she waved off the conversation, still clearly dissatisfied.

I had a long talk with Jesus that night, believe me. "You know, Lord, I don't want to choose between honoring You and what my wife wants. This marriage has to stay intact. I don't want to turn from You, but I've already been through so much. I need You, but I need Deborah, too."

In Full Flame

I had a dream that night—or a vision—I'm not sure what to call it. I dreamed I was in the Shenandoah mountains, and I was with the Lord, and off in the distance was a little flicker of light, a campfire. When I was a Boy Scout I often went camping and you could always see a campfire in the distance, that glimmer of light with its trail of smoke reaching above the tree line. The Lord spoke to me in the dream: "You see that glimmer of light?"

"Yes, Lord, I see it."

He said, "Many ministers run for that fire, and that fire is always off in the distance and they never get there."

He said, "I haven't put you at a distance from the fire. I've put you in the middle of the fire, in full flame. Honor Me with that, because I've given it to you."

I woke up the next morning and looked at my wife and said, "Listen, the Lord gave me this dream last night, Deborah. I'm going to tell you like it is. Here's the dream—please deal with it, because I have to."

That dream changed Deborah's mind. After thinking about it that day, she came to me and said, "Okay. If He's given the Spirit to you like that, then we must honor the Lord. I understand what the Lord is talking about, that many ministers want to run for the fire but the fire remains off in the distance. They haven't been broken like you've been broken, and they'll never achieve that fire. That anointing. You have to honor the Lord. When it's time to give it away, you give it away, and I'll do what I can to help."

Preacher Boy

At the beginning of my second life as a traveling speaker and lay minister, I was also confused about how God wanted me to approach this role. I thought I had to become a "preacher boy," imitating the study habits and speaking style of the evangelists I admired or senior pastors at churches. I started memorizing Scripture like crazy and developing complex outlines. As I delivered the sermons I had so ardently prepared, though, I saw that I was only imitating what full-time preachers could do far better than I.

And I wasn't drawing as deeply as I could on "the hope that is in [me]" (1 Pet. 3:15)—my peculiar vantage point as a doctor and a believer.

I began stoking the fire in ways that made more sense in my circumstances. I drew on what I had learned from David Hogan and his colleagues in Mexico: the most effective preparation starts with praise. Praising the Lord breaks the yoke of darkness. My most powerful sermons or presentations always occur after I spend time praising God. I have praise songs on my laptop computer; wherever I go, before I speak I'll sit in my hotel room for an hour or two, play the praise songs, and I'll walk back and forth across the room, crying out to God, praising Him, and asking Him to minister through me. I'll read passages from the Bible and ask to be led as to what God wants me to say.

This wouldn't prepare me, however, if I didn't read the Bible every day and do my best to begin each morning in prayer. I have to admit I don't have a set pattern. I like to use my computer program to do searches. I use that tool to both go deeper and range widely through the Scriptures as to what the Holy Spirit wants to tell me. At the beginning, I supplemented my reading of the Word with other books, but the longer I do this the more I concentrate just on the Bible. It's always best if I keep my appointment with God at morning's first light, when I'm most free of distractions.

I pray daily for people and, as I mentioned, I fast in preparation for particular challenges. Fasting allows God to confer His power. Our souls encompass the mind, our emotions, and our will, and our spirit comes from God's sustaining presence. The Spirit of God in us battles to communicate with the soul, and the body's demands can interfere. When I "turn off" my body's demands through fasting, the Spirit can better communicate with my soul, and it's easier to accept what God is asking of me.

Excellence

A crucial turning point in this change from "preacher boy" to being more myself came when Pat Robertson invited me to be on the board of Regent University in Virginia. The campus is an oasis of beauty and order—a real witness to God's character. I visited that campus and saw that everything around me was done with such *excellence*. The true meaning of the word met me wherever I turned.

I found myself at the board meeting sitting with people of great accomplishment, who were all Spirit-filled. People like Admiral Vernon Clark, who was in charge of naval operations during the Nixon administration. And Ben Carson, the African-American cardiologist from Johns Hopkins. There were CEOs of gigantic corporations. I had never been in a meeting before where everyone else was a professional and believed in the power of the Holy Spirit and walking in all the gifts of God. I have to admit that in Pentecostal and charismatic circles I have met some weird people, and sometimes there is a theatricality to the services that strikes anyone as contrived. The men and women on Pat Robertson's board affirmed just by their presence that I could be me, as a believer, a scientist, and a physician. The men and women around me were all walking in excellence, and that might have been their greatest witness to God's reality and power.

Through this experience the Lord said clearly to me, "I've called you to be a physician. I haven't called you to be a 'preacher boy.'

I've given you a platform as a physician to win the lost for Christ. You will take this platform and have influence over people, wherever you go, based on your testimony."

I finally understood that many people would find my testimony credible precisely because I was a physician rather than a professional minister.

God Is the Healer, Not Me

Being a physician frees me to take a clear-eyed look at what happens in healing services and to reach out to the unlovely and the destitute. I believe completely in supernatural healing, and I'm clear about God's being the healer, not me. It's not my job to determine who is healed at a meeting and who isn't. All healings are ultimately only signs of God's resurrection power—His promise to raise every believer from the dead to new life in God. God grants these signs or not, according to God's perfect understanding of how best to unite us with God. It's not a matter of believing in just the right way or how much we believe—otherwise, Chad would not be with God right now.

I began to understand both the reality of God's power to heal and His mysterious ways of doing so while Chad was still alive. Part of the way I survived the ordeal of his illness was getting away to crusades to build my faith. One time I went to a Benny Hinn crusade in Nigeria. There were huge crowds of six hundred thousand or more every night. Benny Hinn commissioned twelve of us in his support team to go out into the crowds and pray for the sick.

Almost everyone brought a bottle of anointing oil with him—a precious commodity in Nigeria that probably cost the typical laborer a month's salary. Hundreds came up to me, one after another, wanting to be blessed, prayed for, and anointed. They wanted the whole bottle poured over them.

One family brought a crippled boy who was about six years old. He had never been able to walk. His father brought him to me in his arms. In faith, I suppose, his family had made some crutches for him, with elaborate carvings on the sides. I remember thinking, *Wow, they did a nice job on those crutches!*

The boy's father put him in my arms and asked me to pray for him. "Father God," I said, "in the name of Jesus, I pray over this boy's legs, and I command every ligament, bone, and muscle to work. I command every nerve to be restored, in Jesus' name. I pray healing over him. I pray that he will walk, Lord, in the mighty name of Jesus." I gave him back to his father.

Nothing happened.

I turned to pray for the next person, a white speck in a sea of black faces. All of a sudden I heard the crowd roaring to my right. I turned around and saw this boy's parents kneeling in the dirt, weeping. Then the boy ran past them. He was running back and forth across the field with a great big smile. Not only his parents but everyone from his village was crying—they all knew his story intimately. There must have been two dozen people by his parents, raising their arms and praising God as the boy ran to and fro.

Also at that crusade was a man who had had a stroke. His daughter and son brought him to me. He was drooling. His whole right side was deformed and he couldn't walk. I prayed for him and he was completely restored, and I have a picture of him to prove it.

That night I saw hundreds of kids who were deaf-mutes. One boy had a big hearing aid the size of an old-fashioned matchbox.

After prayer, his hearing returned to normal, and I have a picture of him, too.

Three miracles out of—how many had I prayed for? Upward of a thousand, I think. Sometimes I feel caught between my elation at seeing people healed and my continuing desire that everyone I pray for be restored. It's hard to forget certain faces.

"Show Me Your Glory"

In Nigeria God soon taught me never to make my own reckoning of God's ways. After the crusade was over, all the high-level ministers left. I was sitting in the hotel the following morning—I think it was a Saturday—and the only people left were the crew, who were going out to the site to strike the stage. I didn't want to waste my time in the hotel, so I decided to go out and help the crew. It was a hot day and I was sure they wouldn't mind an extra hand.

I worked at the site until about noon, when I had a break. The sky was bright, piercingly blue. I looked over the field where well over half a million people had gathered the night before, which was now one vast dusty patch of ground. I walked to one side where the grass was still tall, put my hands on my hips, looked up into that bright, bright blue sky, and prayed, "Father God, show me Your glory. Reveal Yourself. Show me Your glory, Father." I was walking through the grass as I prayed, and I tripped.

I looked down and saw that I had tripped over the little boy's crutches—I knew they were his because of the carvings. I was hundreds of yards from where I prayed for him, and the crutches lay in the form of a cross. I started laughing. "Show me Your glory,

Lord?" I realized my own doubts were blinding me to what had been right before me. I lifted up my hands and started praising God. I remembered again how the little boy had been carried to me by his father, and his joy in running for the first time. "You are a great God," I confessed. "Your will be done."

I began walking along in the grass and there were more crutches and canes; in fact, dozens and dozens. The whole grassy field was littered with them! None of the other ministers were there to see this, but God in His mercy wanted me to know that His works far surpass our understanding. The crutches and canes meant that many, many people had been healed. Nigeria is too poor a country for people to throw away such equipment. But those healed had thrown away their crutches in testimony to God's work in their lives.

"Father, show me Your glory." Had He ever!

The Hardest Cases

In 2006 I was at another crusade in London. By this time I was more at ease with God's will in choosing to heal those He chose rather than the ones I would have God choose. And I believed more strongly in God's power to heal the most difficult cases. The need of ministries to lead crusades that make for good television has distorting effects. Often the better-looking people, the well dressed with less-severe ailments, are put in the front benches, so that if anyone is healed from among them, that person can be readily brought to the stage.

The cripples, the demoniacs, the grotesque, and the down-and-out are put in the back, out of camera range. Some ministers justify this by saying that the failure of these hard cases to be healed would cause too much unbelief.

In such circumstances, I make it my policy to go right to the back, because those severely afflicted need the most help. As a physician I undoubtedly find this easier than most, since I see people in bad shape every day. I make it a point to dress in my best three-piece suit and sit among those who are truly "the least of these my brethren" (Matt. 25:40 KJV), those whom disease has robbed of everything but their humanity. I sit there and I pray for the people around me through the entire crusade. (Crusades usually run from three days to a week.)

I was at the back at this crusade in London, where I was assigned to verify people's accounts of miracles. A black woman came up to me and pulled at my jacket. "Doctor," she said, "my son has been healed."

I looked at the infant in her arms, and he seemed far from healed or even well. One quick glance and I concluded that he was suffering from paralysis on his left side. "What do you mean, 'healed'?" I asked, eliciting the woman's story.

The mother and her child had been released from the hospital that day. Her baby had suffered traumatic birth injury and was paralyzed on his left side.

I asked to hold the baby. I pulled his left arm up, it dropped. I lifted up his left leg, it dropped. No movement, no strength, complete paralysis. "I don't see any change here," I said sadly.

"Doctor, I'm telling you, my baby has been healed."

"Why do you think that?"

"The power of God hit me and went through my shoulder, through my arm, where I was holding the baby. The power of God went into my baby. He's been healed."

"Well, let's just keep praying for you."

She looked at me as if she found my doubts far stranger than her story.

I spent some time with her, praying for the child, and later that night, as I was going to sleep, I thought of that child and again prayed for him. Some of those whose experiences I verified were called to the front but not the woman and her child, because from what I could see nothing had happened.

The next night at the crusade, I was again at the back, with all the smelly, dirty, crippled people—my crew. There's something radical in me that wants to see God's power demonstrate itself in the really hard cases, in whose potential healing even those with the stoutest of faiths have trouble believing. I want to see God's greatness. I want to keep believing that one day, by God's grace, the entire back section will be healed!

I felt another tug on my coat—the same woman with her paralyzed child.

"Doctor," she said, "I told you my son was healed last night. Look at my baby now."

I was already gaping at him. Both of the child's arms were up in the air, and he was waving them around like God's orchestra conductor—no doubt leading the heavenly host in a hallelujah chorus. His legs were wiggling. I grabbed the baby's arm, and he pulled it back. His legs were kicking hard enough against my stomach for me to back away. I just burst into tears.

I dropped to my knees. "God, You are real," I prayed. "You showed up. You healed this baby. I saw this baby with my own eyes last night, Lord Father. I saw him. He was crippled. He was totally paralyzed on this side, and now he's restored. Thank You. Thank You."

I said to the woman, "You don't need to go onstage. This baby has been touched by God. Thank you for bringing him to me, because now I've been touched by God, too."

"I'm going to use you now. Watch," God had said. As amazing as these miracles that occurred in distant lands were, what I would see right at home—in my own medical practice—would be even more dramatic.

CHAPTER 12

The Best of Medicine and the Best of Jesus: A New Practice

As I've mentioned, my medical practice is now based on providing my patients with "the best of medicine and the best of Jesus." This can bring astounding results, and I've seen miracle after miracle occur in the lives of my patients.

We start as simply as possible, though, because aiding God's healing in a person's life is not about testing God to see whether God will amaze and delight us with supernatural fireworks. God created us in His image so that we could reason our way to many solutions—as modern medicine shows so well. God expects us to employ all the knowledge that has come through His gifts of reason and imagination to bring about the healing we know He desires.

At the same time, not to understand the spiritual nature of people causes purely secular medicine to miss many opportunities for healing. I would even say that sometimes God grants me spiritual insight as an uncanny diagnostic tool. Although I'm sure some of my colleagues find the way I pray with patients and address their spiritual ills as well as their physical maladies peculiar, I think recognizing the spiritual dimension of people makes me a much better doctor. Also, I've practiced long enough in Palm Beach and lectured widely enough elsewhere for my idiosyncrasies to be tolerated—people know I'm a good doctor.

Many times a patient's way of living needs to be addressed first through medicine and then through a deeper grounding in spiritual reality; there's a bridge that needs to be crossed to health. I tell my patients that we are going to attack their problems with all the weapons at hand, and that we are going to help them cross this bridge, first through medicine and then through true Christian spirituality, to living the healthy, abundant life God wants for everyone.

Some of the most flagrant violators of good health habits are ministers! As with the rest of the American population, their number one killer is heart disease. So when ministers come to me, as they do more and more frequently these days, I tell them that my job is to keep them going for seventy to eighty years—not to let the devil take them out early. I want them to be long-distance runners in winning souls to Christ.

The Word of God says that our bodies are the temple of the Lord (1 Cor. 6:19), and if people are out of shape because of their eating habits and lack of exercise, suffering from hypertension, heart disease, and diabetes, then even if they are ministers they are living in disobedience to God. "It's not about you anymore, brother," I say. "It's about Jesus." I am very direct with them. Most wake up to how much they are putting others' souls in jeopardy as well as their own lives.

So I first administer the best of medicine to my patients who need to get heart-healthy, using medications, regimens of diet and exercise, and interventions when necessary, such as angioplasty and stents. But to bridge these patients totally to health I also need the patients to practice the Word of God in regard to taking care of their bodies. I advise using the prayer practices of praise and thanksgiving, which do wonders for stress. Many times it's possible to take the medications away completely when someone truly changes his or her living and praying habits. That's the final bridge I want patients to cross over.

Spiritual Healing Before Physical

It's also true that an encounter with God may be necessary for those who are profoundly lost before they can begin to heal physically. I take care of many wealthy people, and I often find that their internal gyroscopes no longer work—they don't know how to navigate through life. This comes about in a paradoxical way. Their wealth allows them to manipulate people so easily that soon they don't have real friendships anymore or even genuine relationships with family members. Spirits of division, lust, and perversion take over, and instead of being free as a result of their wealth they are blown about by every whim and fad. First, they stop trusting other people, then they stop trusting themselves, and after that they seem to only know how to seek the next distracting pleasure, and the pleasures have to become ever more exquisite in order to get their attention.

I knew of one man who, dissatisfied with the dimensions of the galley (kitchen) in his yacht, had the oceangoing vessel cut in half so that it could be widened by six feet, at a cost that would have flooded anyone else's balance sheet with red.

Palm Beach does its best to supply diversions to the most jaded. Its many attractions and pleasures can be addictive. When we first moved to town we were plunged into a type of spiritual warfare that I did not understand and hardly suspected. But slowly I began to realize why Paul wrote in 1 Corinthians 1:18–21 that it's very difficult for someone of noble birth, worldly wisdom, or great financial means to enter the kingdom of God. It is foolishness to them.

Faith is not another instrument with which to control the world and manipulate other people, and that's what the spirit of wealth counsels as all-important. Rather, faith is an invitation to live in a much greater reality—that we are not in control but God is. It's only when we recognize our limits that we enjoy the real freedom we do have as a result of being created in God's image. But when we mistake ourselves for gods, we become something less than human.

Serious illness often proves a wake-up call. Many finally realize that all the money, the big houses, the boats, the exotic cars, the young wife or boy toy cannot make them healthy again. At that moment I have the opportunity to intervene and ask, "What is your purpose in life? What is your call? Your legacy? Have you placed yourself and your possession in God's hands? He is real."

When illness reawakens the superrich to reality and they come to Christ, they are radically changed. They experience peace, joy, and a sense of fulfillment and direction—even if their lives will soon be at an end—that they have never known before.

Terminal illness is often a horror, but I've seen God use it to great ends. The suffering someone goes through can prepare the person and even the person's family to meet God.

The secular infatuation with euthanasia is—like the love of money—essentially the worship of one's own will, of being in control. I'm not a fan of hospice care, in general, because hospice often medicates its clients to such a degree that they are deprived of the will to reach out to God. I truly believe that those who advocate medicating people to the point of hastening death or outright euthanasia are playing into the devil's hands, as he does not want people recognizing their standing before God. The devil does not want the seriously ill reaching out for what they most long for, the love of God. I've met few lost people who are not hungry for God and fewer still among this group who do not reach out for Him in their last days.

"I Want to Die"

I had a patient I'll call Elizabeth who was ninety-nine years old. She was a scrawny woman with a hunch to her shoulders that suggested she was about to topple into her grave, but she could still shuffle forward under her own power. Her caretaker, a nurse, came in with her. I had been caring for Elizabeth for about four years, treating her for congestive heart failure.

At the beginning of one appointment, I asked, "Elizabeth, how are you doing?"

"I want to die," she mumbled.

I thought, *Well, you are ninety-nine years old. That makes sense.* But I had my wits about me enough to see an opportunity to ask the all-important question: "If you died, Elizabeth, where would you go? In the afterlife?"

"I'm going to hell."

That caught me off-guard. "What do you mean, you're going to hell?"

"I'm not worthy to go to heaven, so I'm going to hell," she said, resolute if terribly unhappy.

I said, "Elizabeth, not in this office are you going to hell. Do you go to church?"

She was a nominal Catholic. She had not been to church in years.

"That's okay," I said. "It's not about going to church."

"But it is about being worthy, and I'm not!" She was almost shouting at me.

I said, "Elizabeth, if you accept Christ as your Lord and Savior, you will go to heaven. Would you be interested in doing that?"

She said, "Yes, yes I would, but I'm not worthy of doing that and I'm going to hell."

I told her that Christ gave Himself for us because we are all unworthy, and none of us would get into heaven if salvation were not a free gift. "If you accept Christ as your Lord and Savior, as I've said, you can know, right here, right now, that you'll go to heaven. Would you be interested in doing that?"

"Yes," she said, very quietly.

I started leading her in what's often called the Sinner's Prayer, where she could confess to having sinned, acknowledge Jesus' sacrifice as the means of her salvation, and accept Christ as her Savior and Lord.

At the mention of Jesus' name, her teeth clenched and her eyeballs bulged out of her head. I was on one of those little rolling chairs in the exam room, and I scooted over to her. She was sitting in the corner, and I put myself squarely in front of her, with her nurse behind me. I said, "Elizabeth, say this prayer after me, in the name of Jesus."

At the mention of the name, her teeth clenched again in a

way that made her skull virtually protrude through her aged skin—a death mask.

I looked back at the nurse. "What's happening?"

"Every time I mention Jesus she does that, Doctor," she said.

But when I looked back her face was once again relaxed. I tried praying again, with the same result. Her mouth clenched closed; her eyes bulged.

I knew I was dealing with an evil spirit then, so I placed my hand on her crown and forehead and said, "In the name of Jesus, I command you, Satan, to loose this woman. I ask this in Jesus' holy name!"

As soon as I said that, Elizabeth started crying uncontrollably.

Gently I asked, "Elizabeth, can you say the prayer now?"

She nodded. I said, "In the name of Jesus," and she said, "In the name of Jesus," and she continued praying with me, accepting Christ as Savior.

Then her tears really started to flow.

I said, "Elizabeth, you are born again."

She cried all the harder.

"What's wrong, Elizabeth?" I asked.

"Dr. Crandall, for ninety-nine years I've never felt worthy. Right now I'm the happiest I've ever been!" Her sobbing made her chest heave and her hands shake, but she was smiling as the tears rained down.

In Palm Beach and everywhere else over the face of the earth, we are in a battle with Satan. It's often not only a person's sinful will that needs to be addressed but spiritual oppression as well. So sometimes it's the best of medicine and the best of Jesus. At other times, the best of Jesus must come first.

Nickel-Plated Pistol

I had another patient, a man from South America whom I'll call Fred. I had been treating him for years for a number of health issues. He came into the office for an appointment on a Thursday, and he wasn't there so much for my help as to make an announcement.

"Dr. Crandall," Fred said, "I just want to say thank you for everything you've done. But I've made a decision. I'm retired. I've lived my life and done everything I wanted to do. I'm not popular like my wife is—in fact, I don't have many friends. There's no reason for me to live anymore. I went to the gun show at the fairgrounds and bought a used shotgun, and next week I'm going to commit suicide."

His tone was matter-of-fact. He was not asking for my opinion or permission, and I knew how truly serious he was. I told him, "Fred, you are *not* going to commit suicide."

"Yes, I am. I bought the gun. I have it planned."

"No one in my practice is going to commit suicide. Where do you go to church?"

He was a nominal Baptist but had long ceased practicing. "The real question, Fred," I said, "is whether you know Jesus. Do you?"

"No."

"Fred, if you have Jesus in you, you'll be filled with the Holy Spirit and you won't want to commit suicide. You feel lousy, I realize. But what if you were full of peace and joy? You can be."

I started telling him stories of others I had seen come to Christ and preparing him to receive Jesus as Savior. "Fred, why don't

165

you accept Jesus today? Then we'll see if you still want to kill yourself."

"Well, I'll do that, Doctor, but I doubt it's going to change my mind."

We went through the Sinner's Prayer together, as Fred asked Jesus into his life and acknowledged Him as Savior and Lord. I felt that he was praying as sincerely as he was capable, but at the same time his spiritual oppression kept his words from being of much account. I could almost hear the devil whispering to him that this had been a perfunctory exercise. I knew that he needed a dramatic demonstration of God's power to assure him of his salvation and victory over suicide in Christ.

I keep a bottle of anointing oil in each exam room. I went to the shelf where I keep the bottle and poured it over my hands so that they were dripping. I turned around and looked straight at Fred as the fragrance of the oil filled the air. He half turned away, looking at me as if to ask, "What are you doing?"

"You see these hands?" I asked. "These hands are anointed in this oil as a representation of the Holy Spirit. I'm going to put my hand on your forehead, and I'm going to pray that that voice inside you that's telling you to kill yourself will leave. It has to leave if we command it to do so in the name of Jesus. Are you okay with that?"

"Yes." He said this in a tone implying, *Why not? We've come this far.*

I held up my glistening hands and took the couple of steps between us. I repeated, "Fred, I'm going to put my hands on you now, and when I put my hands on you, the power of God is going to hit you, and the oppression you feel is going to leave." I put my dripping hand smack on his forehead and prayed, "Father God, in the name of Jesus, I cast out the spirit of suicide and death in this man, in Jesus' name. I command you to go, Satan. I command you to loose this man, in Jesus' name. Christ releases you, Fred, into His peace and joy. Amen, let it be so, in the mighty name of Jesus."

Fred hopped off the exam table so fast I thought I might have scared him and he was going to run out of the office. *Boom!* He was up. And then he started talking just as fast as he had gotten on his feet. "Dr. Crandall," he said, "that thing that was inside me," he said, "or around me or something—it felt like a horse collar at times, weighted, just pulling me down. That thing I've been feeling so long, it's gone. It is! It's gone." He had a broad smile on his face. "What did you do? It was the prayer, right? And the oil. I don't feel it anymore. It worked. I think it worked. I really do."

Then I became the skeptic. "You sure you feel all right?" I asked.

"All right? I feel great! I'm telling you that thing left me as soon as you prayed. The instant you did."

As a Christian I was rejoicing with Fred, but as a doctor I knew that a little caution might be called for. I wanted to verify if this healing would prove real and lasting, and I wanted to ensure that if Fred needed follow-up psychological care he received it. "Okay, Fred, you see how powerful God really is, don't you?"

"I do, Dr. Crandall, I do."

"Well, let's work with God now and make sure you keep walking with Him and that you are completely delivered from this sense of oppression. It's Thursday. I want to see you back here on Monday. And before you walk out of here I want you to promise me that you won't harm yourself or others in any way. Is that a promise?"

"But it's *gone*. It's just gone."

"Promise?"

"Oh, sure. No question."

On Monday Fred came bounding down the hall like a youngster.

"You look pretty good, Fred," I said. "You still feeling good?"

"I am feeling *great*, Dr. Crandall. When I left your office, you know, I was just so full of joy and peace and happiness and that thing that was weighing me down was just gone, *poof!*, like I told you. When I drove home, I went straight through the front door to my dresser. I grabbed the shotgun, got back in my car, threw the gun in the passenger seat, and drove out near a river. There I heaved the gun into the water. It was all because of that prayer. I've felt like my life could start all over again ever since."

His life did begin again, as Fred is happy and healthy today.

I Doubt My Doubts

These two cases and others like them taught me that many times Satan's oppressive hold over people has to be removed by the power of God before they can be restored to health. I have my credentials as a doctor, and I also have the authority Christ gives His followers to deliver people from spiritual oppression.

At the same time I am always warring against my own doubts, my own skepticism, wondering whether in cases like Fred's his cure might have been the result of his belief in my authority and the dramatic way in which I went about praying for him. But I have been through so many such experiences that I have more doubts of my doubts than of my beliefs. I have learned to walk in the authority Christ gives His followers, and I feel now that when

I see someone suffering from spiritual oppression—someone who is captive to the enemy—I have the authority, like a general in an army, to command the forces of heaven to go into action so that the kingdom of God will come to reign in the person's life.

I hope I'm never presumptuous about this, because I don't have any supernatural power personally. I only know and believe ever more strongly that it's God's will for every person to have God's life in him or her, and that God is pleased whenever His followers help others understand this and, most important, experience it.

CHAPTER 13

Salvation: The Ultimate Healing

At times only God's intervention can help my patients when we've exhausted medicine's resources. But in order for God to heal someone, He has to be present in the patient's life, because that's the primary way God heals us. God addresses our fundamental disease—mortality—in every case when a person asks Christ into his heart. The healing of the soul and the restoration of the person to eternal life with God is the healing He will always work for anyone who believes. God desires souls first and foremost.

We will all die someday, unless Christ returns first. If we are healed of one thing, we will die of something else. But if we have the life of Christ in us, death will be only a transition to a new life with God. When I first started praying for my patients I just concentrated on the immediate problem, the particular disease the patient was battling. God has taught me to address the underlying and eternal issue before asking God to cure a particular illness.

First the healing of the soul and then the healing of the body was definitely the protocol that needed to be followed in Ted Wittimeyer's case. He was a seventy-year-old man I had taken care of for years. He was diabetic and suffered from heart disease and peripheral vascular disease. As a result, he had minimal blood flow in his legs.

Ted came for an appointment one day with a bandage wrapped around his leg. He told me, "Dr. Crandall, they want to cut my leg off next week." I unwrapped the bandage and saw why: he had an ulcer on his leg as big as a cantaloupe that went right down to the bone. "They've been trying to treat this for six months, and it's just not going away." He began to weep. "I don't want to lose my leg. I don't want them to amputate."

I reviewed the doctors he had been seeing with him to make sure he had received the best care. "Ted, you've seen the best doctors in town," I said. "All I can do is pray for your leg, if you'd like me to. Would you like me to do that?"

"You want to pray for me?"

"Yes. But first, you need to become a Christian." I spoke with Ted for a while about his religious training, which was virtually nonexistent. When I asked if he had accepted Christ as Savior, he replied so openly and without any pretense that I thought about the childlike way we all come to Christ. "Is that something I need to do?" Ted asked. If he needed to do that, he would. They were going to chop his leg off. He was desperate.

After Ted received Christ I said, "Now that you've got Christ in you, He's helping to fight the battle. So let's pray for your leg." I put my right hand on the ulcer, in the midst of the goo. "In the name of Jesus, Father God, I cry out for this leg. I ask that You heal this ulcer, in Jesus' name. Lord, we command the tissues to fill in, the muscle, the ligaments, the nerves, the arteries, the veins to be restored in this leg, in Jesus' name. Father God, we command all illness and infirmity to be gone in the mighty name of Jesus. I command you, Satan, to loose this man, in Jesus' name. We command healing on this leg, in the name of Jesus. Lord, peace on this leg, in Jesus' name, amen."

I put a fresh bandage on Ted's leg and met with Ted and his wife in my office study. Ted's wife was naturally anxious about my opinion. "There's no rush on this thing," I said.

"But they want to amputate next week," his wife said.

"I understand that. But let's wait. Come back at the beginning of next week and let me take another look at the ulcer. Perhaps there'll be some improvement." I left it to Ted to explain to his wife what had happened in the office, if he cared to.

Monday, my nurse came running into my office. "Dr. Crandall, you have to speak to Ted's wife. She's on the phone and she's hysterical. I don't exactly know what she's trying to say. She's flipped out."

I went to the nurse's station and picked up the phone. "Dr. Crandall," Mrs. Whittimeyer said, "you're not going to believe this. Fred's at home, and that ulcer, it's starting to fill in with new tissue. The edges of the ulcer are getting smaller, and it's starting to fill in. It's melting away!"

"That's good, isn't it?"

"Sure, it's good. But we're supposed to have the leg amputated this week. What do we do?"

"Like I said, come in and see me. Don't go to the other doctors before you do."

"Okay, we won't."

"Since it's improving, you don't need to see me this week. Let's wait another week. Then come in to me first. Okay?"

Ted came in the next week with a huge smile on his face. He was wearing long pants. He sat on the exam table, both legs covered. I lifted up his pants leg on the one I remembered as being diseased, and there wasn't any ulcer on it. Maybe I had not remembered correctly. I examined the other leg. But there wasn't any ulcer there, either.

It was embarrassing, but I had to ask, "Ted, which leg was the ulcer on?"

"The first one you looked at."

"Take off your pants."

"Dr. Crandall, the ulcer is gone." He was beaming.

"Fine, I believe you, but let me see."

With his pants off I could see that the ulcer had completely filled in with new tissue. It was hyperpigmented, like any major wound that's healed, but otherwise his leg was normal.

I was so incredulous I took a good long look at the other leg to make sure they were both disease-free. I kept looking from one leg to the other, having trouble believing this had actually happened.

Ted's wife was in the exam room with him. "What do you think happened?" I asked.

She said, "God's real. God healed his leg." To this day they're still talking about it and walking with God.

Love Helps People Take the Risk

I am able to talk so openly with people about Christ, in part, because I see them at such vulnerable times in their lives. In my experience, I've had only one patient refuse prayer, a Jewish man suffering from brain tumors who believed his religion forbade him to pray with me. God has given me a great love for the Jews, as I've mentioned before, and particularly ever since Chad's death my Jewish patients have been able—I cannot say exactly why—to sense this. When we are talking about Christ across religious traditions it's vital that the love of Christ be evident within us before we ever say a word.

The love of Christ that He gives us to extend to others touches something very deep within every soul that wants to believe. Perfect love casts out all fear, the Scriptures tell us (1 John 4:18), and when the other person knows we love him or her, the person feels safe and is able to take the risk of faith more easily.

Because we are made in the image of God and made for communion with God, there's always an impulse to reach out for God. It's odd, isn't it, how in times of distress people always call on God, even if in a blasphemous way?

Even before I entered college, I was fascinated by medicine and volunteered as a helper in an emergency room. I wanted to see the gory stuff, the motorcycle accidents, the car crash victims. I couldn't get over how seriously injured people would always call on Jesus for help. One guy's leg was almost cut off in a motorcycle accident. They brought him in in the ambulance without administering any pain medication. He was screaming, "Jesus! Jesus! Jesus!" *Why that name?* I wondered. *Why is he calling on that name?* Small children did this as well.

At the very end, when things are tough, something within us wants to call on the name of God. Most people really do want to know that there is something beyond this life, and if you step forward with that something else, they grab it.

The Big Picture: Mrs. Marion

I had an unforgettable patient who taught me about the big pic-ture—how salvation is the great healing and every physical healing a sign of our ultimate happiness with God. Her name was Mrs. Marion and she came from South Carolina. South Carolinians of Mrs. Marion's stamp have a cultured and musical accent and her refinement showed in everything, from her flowered print dress to the way she held herself. Five years before I had seen Mrs. Marion through a massive heart attack. She was now in her mid-eighties, frail but proud.

"I just came from Charleston with my husband, Mr. Marion," she said with her pleasing formality. "I saw my doctors there and they said I've got pancreatic cancer, and I don't have long to live."

"Really? That's what they said?"

"I came to get your advice. One doctor wants to give me chemo-therapy."

Mrs. Marion was already such a wisp of a woman that I doubted she could survive chemotherapy. "I'm not sure that's a good idea," I said.

"The surgeon—proud of his profession, I imagine, you know how they are—he wants to do surgery."

"Mrs. Marion, I remember what you went through with your heart attack. You won't survive surgery for pancreatic cancer."

"That was my thought. But what should I do?"

"Let me examine you." She lay down on the exam table. I felt her stomach, and she had a tumor the size of a baseball in the mid-dle of her abdomen.

I sat her up. Since she was a Southern belle, I thought she might have a relationship with the Lord, and I asked if she knew Christ. I told her that in my Bible it says that Christians can pray for one another for healing.

"I went to church," she said. "But I never quite understood what people were talking about when they used that kind of language. Not that I'm against it. I simply did not understand."

I spoke with her for quite a while about the true meaning of Christianity.

"I've never had it explained quite so well before," she said. "I would like to be that kind of Christian," she said. "If you'll help me—pray with me, as you've mentioned."

After Mrs. Marion asked Christ into her life, I ran to get one of my nurses, a woman who is a Baptist, and I had her accompany me back into the exam room. I also grabbed my Bible and some anointing oil from my study. I told the nurse, much to her surprise, that she and I were going to pray for Mrs. Marion and her tumor was going to be healed. I rarely experience unusual sensations when praying for someone's healing, but that day I felt on fire—the hair on my arms was standing up. I had an unusual conviction about Mrs. Marion's healing. The nurse had never seen me like this and her eyes were like headlights.

I laid Mrs. Marion down again on the exam table and pulled her dress up to her neck. I said, "Mrs. Marion, I'm going to pray for you in the name of Jesus. I'm going to command that tumor to go in Jesus' name. Are you ready, Mrs. Marion?"

The nurse looked at me as if she wanted to look away but couldn't.

I poured the anointing oil on my hands, and I just whacked right down on the tumor. I said, "In the mighty name of Jesus,

Lord Father, I cry out for the healing of Mrs. Marion." I had my hands on the tumor, and I moved it as I prayed (this didn't cause any pain to the patient). "This tumor must go, in the name of Jesus. I command it to die, in Jesus' name. Satan, you must loose this woman now in the mighty name of Jesus." I kept my hold on the tumor, rattling it back and forth across her abdomen.

Suddenly I felt exhausted as the holy enthusiasm driving me left.

I sat Mrs. Marion up. She was shaking, whether from pure emotion or another sensation I could not tell.

As a doctor, even if I had not been a believer, I would have advised her against either chemotherapy or surgery. Both would only have hastened her death, in my opinion. So I was bold in declaring that all that could be done had been. I said, "Mrs. Marion, it's done."

She was puzzled, of course.

"It's finished. We've done everything the Lord has commanded us to do. You don't need to see the surgeon or the oncologist for chemotherapy. We've prayed for your healing in Jesus' name, and in your case that's all I'd advise."

Mrs. Marion left. My nurse remained in shock the rest of the day.

When Mrs. Marion did not return for a long time, I thought she must have died. I do not presume on the Lord's will—nor would I ever want to. But three months later Mrs. Marion did come back. When my nurse told me she was my next scheduled appointment, I imagined her jaundiced and near death. But then she came walking in wearing one of her floral print dresses, with white low-heeled shoes, accompanied by the estimable Mr. Marion. He walked with a wide shuffle and the help of a cane.

Mrs. Marion sat on my exam table. She had not lost any weight; she looked fantastic.

"How are you doing, Mrs. Marion?" I asked.

"I'm doing great, Dr. Crandall. I just wanted to come by and thank you."

I waited for her to explain why.

"You know, Mr. Marion is getting old, and we're moving back to South Carolina. But we wanted to come by first and thank you. I didn't have chemotherapy. I didn't have surgery. But I was examined a couple of weeks ago and they couldn't find the tumor anymore. It's gone. And I'm believing in the name of Jesus, I'm happy to say."

"Would you mind if I examined you?" I asked.

She lay down on the table. Since she had been recently examined, I simply felt the area over the top of her dress. That hard ball of a tumor was gone. No trace of it. I asked her to sit up.

"You know what I'm going to do now?" she asked. "I'm going to take Mr. Marion home to South Carolina and take care of him."

As I was walking them to the door, Mrs. Marion said, looking up at me with a twinkle in her eye, "You know, you saved my life twice."

"Twice?"

"You remember the heart attack, don't you?"

I nodded. I expected her to make a reference to her pancreatic cancer, but what she said was far more telling. "You remember when you saved my life a second time, don't you? That day when I came to your office and accepted Jesus. You saved my life that day for good when I met the Lord."

Sinning Believers

Christians don't receive as much healing in their lives as they might because of sin. I'm not talking about having what some call the "wrong kind of faith"; I don't want people twisting themselves into mental contortions trying to figure out if they are believing in just the right way as a means of ensuring God will act as they wish. God accepts our faith at whatever level we have it and only desires to give us more. I have seen people with great faith—like Chad—whom God chooses not to heal. On the other hand, many of the healings I've witnessed have been in the lives of people who haven't quite known what to make of God's mercy. At times these people are left wondering, *Why me?* God's ways are far beyond our own.

What I am talking about is serious sin that anyone with a basic knowledge of the Ten Commandments can recognize. A young woman came to see me. She had multiple body complaints. Headaches, aching in her joints, a balky digestive system. No one could quite figure out what was wrong. We did a mega-workup on her and everything came back normal.

With the test results in hand, I sat and talked with her. She was a believer—born again. "I'm sorry," I said, "but I haven't found anything yet. Why don't you tell me more about yourself? Perhaps if we talk for a while, I'll figure out what I'm missing."

"Yes, actually, I'm going away on a trip with my boyfriend."

"Where are you staying?"

"At a hotel, nothing special but close to the beach."

"You're staying at the hotel together?"

"Sure. We live together."

"Can I tell you something? I've looked at everything. I can't find any illness that explains your symptoms. I think you're under spiritual attack, and until you get out of sin this will continue. Living with your boyfriend, having intercourse with him, that's not part of God's plan. You can't be a born-again believer and be living this way. Christians who know God's will and deliberately sin against it are the most miserable people on earth. Far more miserable than atheists. So you need to get out of this relationship or make it a chaste one until you're married. I'm sorry, but you do."

She went away sad because she wasn't willing to change. The truth remains that sin can create illness, psychiatric disorders, heart disease, and many other afflictions. Morality is essentially God's description of the way He intended things to work. When we neglect His "operating instructions," our physical health often starts to suffer.

One of my favorite patients was a salesman named Charles Duke. He was the type who dressed well, could strike up a conversation with anybody, and played a nice round of golf. He was also a charmer and a ladies' man. He had left his wife—who was a believer—and taken up with a younger woman. They were living what they took to be the good life in Florida.

Despite all this, he was a believer, albeit a big-time backslider. I took care of him over a number of years, and almost every time I saw him I tried to say something about turning back to the Lord. Once divorced from his wife, he still refused to marry the woman with whom he was living. I told him this wasn't right. "If you are going to live with her, you need to marry her."

"Oh, Chauncey," he'd say. "I'm just not ready for all that."

I had not seen him for more than a year when one day he came to the office, thin, in fact down to skin and bone, his body eaten up and wasted. He brought his X-rays in. "Doc, I've got cancer." He started weeping.

I looked at his X-rays and saw a big tumor at the top of his left lung. There wasn't anything left to do for him but pray, and I told him so. "All I can do is take you to a healing service tonight, if you'll go."

He said, "I turned from God, and I can't believe this happened."

"Don't you think it's time you started believing again?"

He said he would go with me that night to the healing service. We went to a church close by. During the service, the power of God hit him, and he dropped to his knees crying. A bunch of us were around him, praying for him.

The following week, he called me up. "Listen, Doc, something happened at that meeting."

"I'm sure it did," I said.

"No," he said, "you don't understand. I'm healed. I know I'm healed. I want you to do another CT scan this week."

"It's too early. Your insurance will not cover another one so soon."

"Well, I'm telling you, Doc, I was touched. I was healed."

"Okay. When it's time, you can have another scan and we'll find out."

The following week, on a Thursday, Charles had another scan and showed up in my office without an appointment on Friday, the CT scan results under his arm. He said, "I want you to tell me what happened."

I was thinking he wanted me to interpret the scan results,

probably in a more positive way than the first doctor, who told him the unhappy truth. I thought the tumor would still be there when I held the image up to the light. But the tumor was gone. Completely gone. His lung tissue looked absolutely normal.

I said, "Stay here, Charles. Let me go and call the radiologist." I placed the phone call. "Listen, I'm calling about Duke. Can you pull up the old films on the computer, and the new films, and tell me what's going on?"

He went over the old film, which clearly showed an apical cancerous tumor on his left lung.

"What about the new ones?" I asked.

"Crandall, there's no tumor on this X-ray. What did you do to him?"

I said, "Are you sure? You're looking at the right guy?"

"I'm sure. I've got the dates and everything right before me."

I went back to the exam room where Charles was waiting.

"What did you find?"

I looked straight at him. "The blood of Christ has healed you, Charles. Your tumor is gone."

He dropped to his knees right there in my exam room, weeping and even shrieking, crying out to God: "Lord, I'm sorry I turned from You! I'm sorry, God!" He was screaming this aloud in my office! He was just totally amazed.

When he stood up, a little rocky from so much emotion, he mumbled once more, "He healed me. I've turned from Him and run from Him for so many years, and all I had to do was cry out to Him and He showed up. Can you believe it?"

He went home and got married.

The Gift of Tongues and the Gift of Life

Personally, I find the greatest thing about participating in God's healing is the way in which it draws me closer to God; how it deepens my understanding, trust, and love of God. It's truly a gift to be used by God in this way, and in my case it brought along with it other spiritual gifts as well.

When Chad was ill, we started going to a church where people prayed in tongues. I started researching this phenomenon in the Bible and praying about it. "Lord, if this is a true gift, please let me receive it. I need it. I'm in a battle."

For months and months I was crying out to God with this request. "If it's real, I want it. If it's not, that's okay, too." I'd be praying as I drove my car to work, and I'd start mumbling and jumbling syllables, hoping to prime the pump. But I knew all of this was coming from me. I had not truly received this baptism of the Holy Spirit. And the more I prayed about it, the more I wanted it. At the same time I had my doubts, because some of the people in our new church were pretty strange. It would be a long time before I had fellowship with other professionals who spoke in tongues, like those who sit on Pat Robertson's board.

Then one day I was in the hospital and this lady came into the emergency room with a massive heart attack. They called me. "Listen, Crandall, you need to take her to the operating room. This woman is dying. She's had a severe anterior wall myocardial infarction."

So we sent her to the operating room, and my team and I scrubbed in. In that situation I'm like the conductor of an orchestra. Everyone knows where he or she is supposed to go and what his or her job is, but I have to lead one very hectic orchestra. I was standing over this woman, working catheters through her groin to the heart, inserting stents, trying to get her blood pressure up. We started IVs and hit her with atropine, epinephrine, and the clot-dissolving drugs called thrombolytics. We were trying to abort the heart attack by going in and helping the artery open itself up. But as we worked on her, death entered the operating room and her heart flatlined.

All of a sudden my hands went up in the air, uncontrollably. There I was with my arms raised, dressed in my scrub suit, with my mask on. I had no control over my arms. And I started speaking this unknown language. This river of a language I didn't understand started pouring out of my mouth. I thought, *I can think, I can see, I can hear, but I have no control over what is coming out of my mouth.* And I still had no control over my hands, which were hovering in the air over her body. This was embarrassing and I tried to put my hands down, but I couldn't. I continued mumbling an uncontrollable river of language that I'm as far from understanding now as I was then. I could only wonder, *What is going on?*

I looked at the nurses, and they were sure looking at me. They were waiting for me to give them further instructions, but all I could do was pray in a language I did not understand. I noticed that the words I was speaking came from deep down inside, rolling out, coming out of my belly. My brain did not have anything to do with it. Again, I could think. I could see. I could hear. But I couldn't control what I was saying and I couldn't bring my arms down. This went on for what seemed forever, although probably no longer than three to five minutes.

All this time the heart monitor was sounding the piercing note that declares a patient has flatlined. Then a heartbeat came back.

Then another heartbeat, and then the first perfect one. After about a dozen perfect heartbeats, I was able to put my arms down and speak normally. One nurse patted my sweating brow and another asked if I was okay. "What were you doing?" they asked.

"I was just crying out for this lady's life, in Jesus' name." It was all I could think to say.

I ran to the head of the table, wanting to look at her eyes to see if they were fixed, dilated. Her eyes were normal. She started to blink. I went back and finished inserting the stents. The patient remained stable.

In fact, she recovered very well and soon left the hospital. The nurses kept asking me about what had happened. "Listen, I don't know," I said. "God must have taken over for a couple of minutes."

Some months later, my missionary friend from Colombia, Andrew McMillan, came to see me. We fell into a pattern of watching for revivals breaking out in Florida, and when God seemed to be on the move in one place or another, I'd call Andrew up and we'd go to these meetings whenever possible. I was hungry for the move of God and so was he.

We were driving across the state of Florida one night, on the central highway known as Alligator Alley. The middle of the state looks just like Africa, with savannah all around and isolated stands of trees. We were headed to the other side of the state where a revival was going on. We started talking about Reinhard Bonnke's videotape *Raised from the Dead*, a documentary about a man who came back to life even after having been embalmed. There were few cars on the highway. We had praise music on and felt the spirit of God's presence. I said, "Wouldn't it be great if we could pray for someone and see them rise from the dead? It would elevate my faith like nothing else."

The Lord spoke to me audibly. This wasn't a feeling; it was a voice. "Don't you remember that woman? When you received the gift of tongues?"

I said, "Yes, Lord."

"If I hadn't been there that day and spoken through you, she would have died. But because you received the gift of ecstatic tongues, she was raised from the dead."

Once I had sufficiently recovered to speak at all, I told Andrew about the experience, praying over my patient in tongues while her heart flatlined. "Andrew, whenever I've thought of that since, I've only thought about receiving the gift of tongues. I hadn't thought until now that I'd seen the dead raised."

CHAPTER 14

Raising the Dead: The Rest of the Story

I've been privileged to be part of raising the dead twice, then; the first time at the moment I received the gift of tongues and later in the celebrated case of Jeff Markin, with which we began.

God's raising of Jesus is the foundation of the Christian faith. We do find it extraordinary, though, even when we believe in it, because we see God's purposes too narrowly in terms of our own points of view. That's why it's important to say that I've been a part—only one part—of God's raising of the dead. In the case of Jeff Markin, my own understanding of what had transpired in his life kept enlarging over the course of his treatment.

After Jeff came back to life in the emergency room, we rushed him down to the intensive care unit. The buzz of what had happened filled the place—everywhere people were whispering. "Did you hear what happened? This guy was dead and he came back!" "Look how cyanotic his fingers and toes are. The nurse said she was prepping him for the morgue!" "Crandall comes in, prays over the guy, they hit him with the paddles one more time…and *bam!* He comes back, after being down more than forty minutes."

"Yeah, it'll be a nice life as a vegetable," the skeptics wagged.

"Who knows?" others countered. "Who knows anything after this?"

The miracle of Jeff's coming back from the dead occurred on a Friday. I was off that weekend and transferred his care to one of my partners, Gabe. I remember finishing up my orders for his care with a note: "Gabe, this guy came in and died, and I prayed for him, and he came back to life. God must have a call on his life, so there's nothing you can do to kill him over the weekend."

Despite this bravado, I had my doubts and was rattled by what had happened. I had a meeting late Friday afternoon with a banker, a Christian friend, and I couldn't help spilling out the story. My friend could hardly believe what I was telling him, but I could see he was tucking away the information.

A Vision of Hell

On Monday when I arrived at the hospital, as I've mentioned, I expected Jeff Markin to be unconscious. I was about as surprised as anyone to find him alert and talking. Then I truly became curious. What had he experienced? Seen? Known?

"Jeff," I asked, "where were you that day? I prayed over your body, but I really thought you had gone. Where were you? I mean, did you have an out-of-body experience? What was it like?"

"Dr. Crandall," he said, "I'm so disappointed." He shook his head back and forth and kept shaking it. "I'm so disappointed."

"About what?"

"No one came to visit me."

"What do you mean, 'No one came to visit' you?" I asked, wondering if he was as coherent as he looked.

As he described what he had experienced, I would become more and more convinced that he was indeed coherent, but he had experienced something or been given a vision of something that comes only with death. "I was in a casket," he said, "in a dark room for eternity—hell, okay? My family didn't come, my coworkers didn't come, my buddies, no one. I sat there for eternity, alone. In total darkness. I'm so disappointed. I'm so disappointed." He kept repeating that last phrase over and over.

Finally, I broke in. "Did anything ever happen?"

"After being there for eternity," he said, "some men came in and they wrapped me up and they threw me in the trash."

Being thrown in the trash might have sounded too simple or anticlimactic to some, but it made me think of how Jesus had used Jerusalem's waste dump—Gehenna—as an image of hell.[1] Being thrown away as useless and unwanted can only be hell for men and women who are created to enjoy God's love and life for eternity. Being thrown in the trash is a great description of the eternal separation from God that constitutes hell.

Through Christ I had the antidote to Jeff's vision of final separation—the total waste of his life. I asked him if he knew Jesus.

His ex-wife was a Christian, he said. She turned to Christ twenty years before, and he left his family rather than submit his will to Christ's. He knew about being born again. He had once decided against it.

I said, "Jeff, if you'll accept the Lord now as your Savior, you will never again be thrown in the trash. There must be a call on your life for God to bring you back. Will you accept Jesus today?"

He said he would. I grabbed his hand, and we prayed together for God to fill Jeff with God's everlasting life. When God called again, Jeff would be prepared to meet Him. Jeff became a Christian right there in his hospital bed, repenting of his sins, receiving Christ as Savior, tears rolling down his cheeks. He was born again.

Responding to Pain with Love

Jeff's acceptance of Jesus was the ultimate miracle in his life—one that had been prepared by many, many prayers before mine. When I went home that evening, I received a telephone call from my friend the banker. He said, "Dr. Crandall, you are not going to believe this. After our talk, I went home and told my wife the story of the man who came back from the dead. She works at a Christian school. She told a woman who is her coworker there. The coworker dropped to her knees. 'Do you know who that man is?' she asked. 'He's my ex-husband. Twenty years ago he left me and our two children because I accepted the Lord as Savior. I was going the way of Jesus, and he decided he didn't want that and left the family. For twenty years I've been praying for his salvation.'"

Later, I also found out that Jeff's daughter had been in the parking lot that day. She knew her father was being treated in the emergency room. She didn't know he had been declared dead. She was crying out to God for his life—his eternal life. She prayed, "I was born in that hospital, Lord. May my father be born again in the same hospital."

The whole picture, one truer to the ways of God, started coming together for me. God works through His people to bring about the reign of God, the kingdom of God, in the lives of individuals. As people are transformed, so are the families and the places and the cultures in which they live. God's love goes out in ever-widening circles. We participate in this life-giving process through entering into the mystery of Christ's suffering. It's ultimately all about Christ's resurrection, yes, but first of all it's about Christ's cross.

An ex-wife responds to her husband's desertion of the family not with bitterness but with prayers for his salvation for twenty years. She responds to the suffering he has inflicted with love. The daughter the man left to be raised alone by her mother does not turn her back on her father; instead she maintains a relationship and prays for his salvation. Like her mother, she responds to desertion with love.

This leads to the intervention of a doctor who, by turning toward God rather than away from Him at the moment of his son's death, receives a special anointing for healing prayer. This "just happens" to be the doctor who is called into the emergency room to oversee this man's care after a heart attack. A doctor who takes the risk of looking foolish and obeys God's direction to join his prayer to the many prayers of the family for the salvation of this man, Jeff Markin. In this way Christ's cross and resurrection triumph through those who by faith join their wills to Christ's and walk the same difficult path.

The story of Jeff Markin shows how the work of healing prayer belongs not to me but Christ, and through Christ it belongs to *all* those who believe. As believers, it's *our* work as Christ's body in the world. What I have to say would only be a curiosity if it were about unusual events in my life. The true meaning of the story I've been telling lies in its common application. God calls *everyone* into the work of restoring the world through Christ's cross and resurrection. He calls *everyone* to respond to the world's evil with His love, which allows, at times, for miraculous healings as signs that God will ultimately defeat death itself. That as members of God's family we will be resurrected to new life; to a new heaven and a new earth, where every tear will be wiped away, every sorrow. Where we will be happy the way we are when the impossible comes true and the dead come back to life.

Why Me?

The rest of Jeff's story, to date, underlines how miracles are one means by which God draws people into a relationship. So many fine Christians pray for God's healing and are not healed in this life, just like Chad. (We know by faith they are healed, nevertheless, when they pass through death into God's presence.) On the other hand, God can grant such favors as signs of His love, even when that love is not being reciprocated. While Jeff's healing made perfect sense to the Christians around him, the miracle at times puzzled Jeff. *Who am I?* he asked. He was not educated, a person of influence. He certainly didn't deserve the miracle in terms of his own behavior. He was living in unbelief when he was miraculously healed.

Miracles are not about who we are or what we deserve. They are about how God sees us and what God wants for us. God loves us and He draws us through showing us how much He loves us—at times through miracles. At one point, almost in desperation, Jesus said, "Believe me when I say that I am in the Father and the Father is in me; or at least believe on the evidence of the miracles themselves. I tell you the truth, anyone who has faith in me will do what I have been doing. He will do even greater things than these" (John 14:11–12).

Jeff began maturing in the faith, worshiping regularly and participating in a Bible study. Who knows what God has in store for Jeff now? Only this, that God is jealous of Jeff's love and wants to draw Jeff closer and closer to Him. This is God's essential will for all of us. We may experience miracles of healing or we may not— either way, strangely, that's no guarantee of belief. On one occasion nine of the ten lepers Jesus healed went away without a word of thanks (Luke 17:11–19).

If we reach out to God in faith, though, we will most certainly experience the ultimate miracle of God's love.

CHAPTER 15

The Story Goes Global

I never thought that the story of Jeff Markin's healing would garner worldwide attention. But God's purposes are always far beyond our own, and God works with both a shocking profligacy and economy at the same time. God performs a miracle when it's least expected, then takes this sign and uses it as a chess master would to resolve a thousand possible moves and countermoves with one stroke.

An invitation came from the World Christian Doctors Network to submit a case study of God's miraculous work to their fourth annual conference in Miami. I asked my colleague Jeremy McKeen, whom I had brought into my practice as a chaplain, to write up what had happened in Jeff's case and submit it for consideration. Once Jeremy's summary of the case landed, the phone started ringing off the hook. This surprised me, but I was happy to attend the conference and document Jeff's healing. I appeared there on Friday, July 13, 2007.

At the beginning the conference threatened to be a little too matter-of-fact, with doctors presenting one case after another. I was sitting at a cafeteria table, the second one back from the podium, waiting for my turn to present. I was becoming impatient, actually, with the general lack of enthusiasm, as I felt we should be testifying to God's glory without so much professional detachment.

Then a Korean music team came out, six young women who played violins. They began playing praise music masterfully. I could not help but think of Chad, naturally, as he had become so adept at the violin so quickly. My friend the minister Joel Stockstill was also an expert violinist. The music recalled all that I had been through with Chad, and the Holy Spirit used the music to release emotions and heal my grief. I started weeping and wailing in this conference. I wasn't crying softly. I let it all out: *Aaaahhhh-hhhhhhh!* The more I wailed, the better I felt. I let loose for about fifteen minutes while these magnificent young women played. People came around me, patted me on the back, and asked if I was okay. I was being purged clean by the Holy Spirit, who was restoring *my* spirit, making it fresh and new.

The master of ceremonies then announced that Dr. Crandall would be presenting his case, having no idea Dr. Crandall was the basket case in the second row. I could hardly stand and make my way to the stage, but I had at that moment an unbelievable anointing of the Holy Spirit.

At the podium, I started to present what happened with Jeff Markin. I had a video presentation as further evidence. As I told the story, the detached professionals in the audience became engaged and shouted affirmation. They were cheering and clapping. As I summarized, I said, "Who at this conference wants to raise the dead in Jesus' name? Isn't that what we are called to?"

The whole place stood up, praising God—it was electric. Then they began to come forward for prayer. Nothing like this had ever happened at the conference. I started praying for people individually, and they were touched left and right.

The Lord had it all planned. He knew when they were going to call me up. He knew I needed to be slammed by the Holy Spirit right before. He prepared me and my audience to open our eyes to the wonder He had performed in Jeff Markin's case.

The Lord also placed Dan Wooding from ASSIST News in the audience. For many years Dan reported on Billy Graham's crusades. He wrote up Jeff's story and sent it to all the news outlets.

The story was picked up by the local Fox TV affiliate and then Fox produced a segment on the story for a national Christmas special. Online videos about Jeff Markin's healing have now been accessed millions of times.

A Consuming Fire

Once a humdrum Christian, I now experience my faith as a consuming fire. I want every moment of every day to be devoted to advancing the kingdom of God. My wife, Deborah, and I try not to be drawn to the world anymore. God has given us everything, we feel. He's opened up the heavens. Our only questions are *How do we serve Him today?* and *Which direction would God have us go?*

From all that's happened, I know that wherever I go the Holy Spirit goes with me and speaks through me. Everything must be consumed by this fire of God. I used to think about how I could advance in medicine, acquire wealth, and so forth. Now I think only about how I can advance in the Lord and do the Lord's work. One step off that narrow path and Deborah and I both begin to notice. Our anxiety levels rise. When we are utterly devoted to the Lord, the work becomes easy. It's not a burden. When someone wants to work for the Lord, the Lord opens the doors. His burden is light.

Many people I pray for are not healed, of course. I let that be the Lord's business. I don't stop. I keep going, on to the next battle. If one battle's not won, I don't let that discourage me. I've learned how to battle, how to pray, how to keep walking in faith. As I've done so, praying for people has become more and more natural. I have faith that God is real, and that God will show up. So I pray with authority. I pray with boldness. And I carry the fire of God. God has given me the gift of healing in order to keep me standing in His holy fire, to keep me in full blaze.

My number one desire is to gather souls into God's kingdom. It's not to heal people, as important as that is. I'm after your soul, for Jesus, in Christ's name. That's my mission. It's one that I feel Chad joins me in, as his suffering and death were the means God used to give me a share in Christ's cross. So as I reach out to those million souls I asked for in exchange for Chad's life, I think of the life Chad and I, Christian and I, Deborah and I, and all the people of God will ultimately share together for eternity.

I invite you to become a follower of Christ or to become "radicalized" in your Christian walk. As in Jeff Markin's case or in that of my patient Elizabeth, who feared hell would be her eternal destiny, it doesn't matter where you find yourself in life. The Bible says that if we confess our sins, God through Jesus Christ will forgive us and make us right and whole (1 John 1:9). It proclaims,

"Believe in the Lord Jesus, and you will be saved" (Acts 16:31). Jesus Christ Himself assures us that the *work* of God is to *believe* in Him. You can begin a relationship with Christ right now through the simplest of prayers. Confess your sins and ask Jesus to forgive you, acknowledge Him as your Savior and Lord, and pledge that you will follow Him as long as your life will last.

If you are a humdrum Christian as I was, don't wait until you are confronted with an ultimate test of faith like a child's illness to learn how to fight the battle. You are in a war! You need to be in training every day, with constant prayer and times for fasting. You need to "put on the whole armor of God" (Eph. 6:11 KJV) by immersing yourself in the Scriptures and putting all your gifts and talents at God's disposal. Following after Christ will entail offering whatever suffering God allows in your life back to God for the redemption or betterment of the world. Will you be able to do this? Will you count suffering for Christ as a privilege? That takes a degree of spiritual maturity that you just won't have unless you prepare yourself in advance.

I pray for you. I pray for all your hurts and wounds and illnesses and those of the people you love. I pray that God will heal you now through Jesus Christ our Lord!

I pray for the griefs that you bear—the loss of children, of parents, of husbands and wives, of brothers and sisters and dear friends. I pray for you in whatever loneliness and fear you may be experiencing, in whatever trouble. May God heal you of all your distress, removing every sorrow, wiping away every tear.

I pray that the glory of God will be upon you, that Christ will be in your heart so that it's bursting with joy, that the Holy Spirit will dwell within you with a power you've never known before.

And I pray with confidence, because in Christ every promise is yes! (2 Cor. 1:20). The deepest longings of our hearts will all be fulfilled, as God raises us from death to life. "Why should any of you consider it incredible that God raises the dead?" (Acts 26:8). I've seen it with my own eyes and I know that if you have faith in Christ, you will as well. Amen and amen!

Acknowledgments

I would like to thank those who supported me as I "ran after Jesus for everything he could give me"—many of the Lord's gifts came through these men and women.

I cannot fail to mention God's ministers who taught me and prayed with me, especially David Hogan, Joel Stockstill, Charles and Frances Hunter, Reinhard Bonnke, Andrew McMillan, Greg Rider, and Tom Mullins. Many others prayed with my wife, Deborah, and me, and I want them all to know that their prayers were answered because "no matter how many promises God has made, they are 'Yes' in Christ" (2 Cor. 1:20).

I received invaluable assistance in developing the manuscript from several talented publishing professionals. Thanks go to the staff at FaithWords, especially my editor Joey Paul. Joey took the time to get to know me personally and helped me think through how I could be most effective as an author and speaker. Holly

Halverson provided detailed editorial assistance, making sure the manuscript would have the greatest possible impact and stand up to scrutiny.

My assistants Jeremy McKeen and Peter Mariades made extremely helpful contributions to the project at various stages. I could not have carried on my practice, my active speaking schedule, and completed this book project without the work of these two fine men.

I am indebted more than I can say to my literary agent, Sealy Yates, who saw the book's potential and enabled the project to go forward at a difficult stage. Thanks for getting the project on the right track, Sealy.

Finally, I'd like to thank Harold Fickett, my book doctor, who cared for the story's beating heart.

Notes

Chapter 4

1. Brian J. Druker, MD, et al., "Activity of a Specific Inhibitor of the BCR-ABL Tyrosine Kinase in the Blast Crisis of Chronic Myeloid Leukemia and Acute Lymphoblastic Leukemia with the Philadelphia Chromosome," *New England Journal of Medicine* 344 (April 5, 2001): 14.

Chapter 7

1. Niki Foster, "Who Is J. M. Barrie?" www.wisegeek.com/who-is-j-m-barrie.htm.
2. http://en.wikipedia.org/wiki/Pan_(god), http://en.wikipedia.org/wiki/Panic, http://www.knowledgerush.com/kr/encyclopedia/Pan_(god)/, http://en.wikipedia.org/wiki/J._M._Barrie.
3. See Lyn Gardner, "Confronting Peter Pan's 'Awfully Big Adventure,'" http://www.theage.com.au/articles/2002/12/29/1040511254669.html.

Chapter 8

1. Kevin Hrebick and Adrienne S. Gaines, "Church-Growth Strategy Goes Global," Charisma, http://charismamag.com/index.php/component/content/article/248-people-events/7978-church-growth-strategy-goes-global--?format=pdf.

Chapter 14

1. See http://en.wikipedia.org/wiki/Gehenna.